Praise for
Power to the People:
The New Road to Freedom and Prosperity for the Poor, Seniors and Those Most in Need of the World's Best Health Care

Peter Ferrara is delightfully eccentric, wicked smart, and laser focused and his book, *Power to the People*, is a must read. I urge everyone, especially members of Congress, to pay attention to what Ferrara has to say.
— Arthur B. Laffer, Ph.D.
Laffer Associates

Here you succinctly have everything the next president and Congress needs to positively reform entitlements in ways that will enable people to enjoy a far better life and enable the U.S. to achieve a more vibrant economy. An inspiring achievement.
— Steve Forbes
Chairman and Editor-in-Chief
Forbes Media

Using pro-growth, free-market incentive principles, Peter Ferrara has come up with a set of dynamic entitlement reforms that every presidential candidate should embrace.
— Larry Kudlow
Senior Contributor, CNBC

This book should be called "The Solution." It tackles the major threats to our future – both our prosperity and our liberty – and shows how we can do a U-turn away from our present path down the road to serfdom. Peter Ferrara clearly and convincingly explains that reforms to our nation's entitlement spending can avoid the slow-motion train wreck of Greece and Detroit while opening the door to an explosion of individual liberty and prosperity.
— Grover Norquist
President
Americans for Tax Reform

Power to the People should be the next president's GPS system to getting America back on the path to rising incomes and declining deficits.

— Steve Moore
Distinguished Visiting Fellow
The Heritage Foundation

What's key about Ferrara's new book is that he reminds his readers of the potential for growth, higher living standards, and improved individual wellbeing that comes with modernizing outdated entitlement programs that threaten to suffocate America's dynamism. Ferrara rejects the false notion that entitlement reform is much pain for little gain. *Power to the People* reveals the enormous upside to reforming government health care and retirement programs so they enable individuals to exercise more choice and responsibility.

— Romina Boccia
Grover M. Hermann Research Fellow
The Heritage Foundation

Power to the People

The New Road to Freedom and Prosperity for the Poor, Seniors, and Those Most in Need of the World's Best Health Care

Peter J. Ferrara

The Heartland Institute
www.heartland.org

Published by The Heartland Institute
3939 North Wilke Road
Arlington Heights, Illinois 60004
phone 312/377-4000
fax 312/377-5000
www.heartland.org

Additional copies of this book are available from
The Heartland Institute for the following prices:

1-10 copies	$12.95 per copy
11-50 copies	$10.95 per copy
51-100 copies	$8.95 per copy
101 or more	$6.95 per copy

Printed in the United States of America
ISBN-13 978-1-934791-53-0
ISBN-10 1-934791-53-9

Manufactured in the United States of America

Contents

1

Introduction

The greatest fallacy in public policy today is the failure to see the vast, pro-growth opportunities offered by fundamental, structural entitlement reform.

Today's entitlement programs broadly discourage capital formation, investment, and labor force participation. Structural reforms that would reverse those effects would pump huge waves of capital and labor into the economy, creating an economic boom.

The failure of the nation's entitlement system cries out for an entirely new approach. Instead of the negative politics of cutting benefits for the poor, seniors, and those who need health care, the productivity and market incentives of pro-growth entitlement reform would result in better benefits and incomes for the poor and seniors, and better health care for the sick. At the same time, pro-growth entitlement reform would reduce taxes and government spending by the greatest amounts in world history.

This book presents a comprehensive entitlement reform agenda. These reforms are all positive and populist, producing far better results for the poor, seniors, and those who need health care. They rely on modern capital and labor markets, and market incentives and competition, to achieve the social goals of the current entitlement programs. Markets, incentives, and competition naturally work far better at achieving those social goals than government-monopoly tax and redistribution programs.

In addition, these reforms over a generation would reduce federal taxes and spending by at least half from what they would be otherwise. They are all proven reforms that have already been tried and have worked spectacularly in the real world. These reforms would contribute to far greater economic growth and prosperity for all.

Indeed, these reforms can eliminate involuntary poverty, assure universal health care, and empower middle-income working people to retire as millionaires. They can produce decades of booming economic growth significantly above the historic, world-leading, postwar American economic growth trend line, which made America the mightiest economic and military power in world history.

This reform platform builds on ideas propounded by Milton Friedman and Art Laffer, the two greatest economists of the twentieth century, and President Ronald Reagan, the most visionary and insightful political leader of that century. I had the privilege of working for President Reagan directly as a young man recently out of Harvard Law School, in the White House Office of Policy Development. I learned these ideas as that young man sitting for long talks with Reagan's top welfare policy advisor, the wise, shrewd, and astute Robert Carleson.

This reform vision was developed over the past 35 years through my work at the Reagan White House, The Heritage Foundation, the Cato Institute, and now The Heartland Institute, as well as other free-market institutions and organizations over the years.

The Problem, and the Opportunity

Soon after World War II, U.S. federal government spending as a percent of gross domestic product (GDP) stabilized at around 20 percent. It remained there until President Barack Obama took office. That period covered close to two-thirds of a century.

All of the great debates, the political crusades, the battles between left and right, the liberal War on Poverty, the steady rise of entitlement spending, the Reagan revolution – all of these together merely held federal spending in equipoise during this entire period, ultimately growing no faster than our enormously productive economy grew over the same period.

Until recently.

The Congressional Budget Office (CBO) projects that on our current course, under current policies, federal spending would soar to 30 percent of GDP by 2027, 40 percent by 2040, 50 percent by 2060, and 80 percent by 2080. Add in state and local government spending, and we are literally on a course toward full-blown communism, where the government takes and spends everything the economy produces.

Obama has exacerbated and accelerated the problem. Federal spending soared to 25 percent of GDP in his first year in office, breaking through the long-term, bipartisan consensus. As a U.S. senator, Obama voted for the bloated budget that prevailed in his presidency's first year.

But the long-term growth of federal government spending is not primarily due to Obama. It is due to the long-term expansion in our nation's entitlement programs. That is why it was so reckless and irresponsible to pass Obamacare, which adopted or expanded three entitlement programs, adding napalm to the fire.

I don't believe in allowing unnecessary human suffering. Conservatives and enlightened free-market advocates understand and embrace the injunction of Friedrich Hayek, the founder of modern libertarianism, in favor of social safety nets to prevent material deprivation. That injunction was picked up and developed into a modern and highly appealing political platform by Jack Kemp, who knew how to put the political words to social music and liberate the advocates of freedom and prosperity to dance and sing.

This vision was embraced by Reagan, who knew his country and the American people. He was a convictions politician firmly planted on principle but devoted to an uplifting vision rooted in the American Dream, consonant with the hopes and aspirations of average working people inspired to come to and develop this then-wilderness land by just such an elevated vision of freedom and prosperity for all.

It was handed off to the visionary Newt Gingrich, who knows a winning, enlightened idea when he sees it. He propagated that vision to extend the Reagan Revolution to Congress, where he enshrined what has proven to be durable majorities.

The fundamental problem is that America's current entitlement programs are based on old-fashioned tax-and-redistribution models dating to late nineteenth century Old World Europe. Instead of trying to address the entitlement crisis by raising taxes and cutting benefits, we need to think outside the box and advance fundamental, structural reforms that would transform the programs to rely primarily on modern capital and labor markets, with positive, pro-growth incentives. This involves extending supply-side principles to the incentives of essential social safety nets, to structure those programs to maximize effectiveness, economic growth, and national prosperity.

The lessons here for free-market and Tea Party activists are first that government spending can be reduced by far more through structural reform than by simple-mindedly slashing benefits for the poor, retired working people, and those in need of the best health care. Second, safety nets built on the foundation of markets, incentives, and competition, rather than government monopoly, taxation, and redistribution, would not be an onerous burden on the economy and working families, especially in the context of a comprehensive program of pro-growth economic policies. Milton Friedman was not noted for railing against benefits for the poor, retired working people, and those in need of essential health care, but for policies that would maximize economic growth and prosperity. This vision has been further developed by the intellectual leaders of supply-side economics, such as Art Laffer and Steve Moore.

This inherent decency of intent combined with strategic wisdom is why the trailblazing work of these intellectual pioneers was so readily and successfully propagated by effective political leaders such as Reagan, Kemp, and Gingrich.

Broken Current System

The current entitlement programs based on tax and redistribution detract from economic growth and prosperity by creating incentives that produce counterproductive behaviors. The nation's welfare programs create powerful incentives not to work because they provide a free income without working. Indeed, working and earning income disqualifies one from eligibility for the free benefits. Taxpayers are consequently paying the bottom 20 percent of the income distribution literally a trillion dollars a year not to work. For that kind of money they are more than willing to do as asked, which removes them from contributing to the economy.

Not working is counterproductive for the poor themselves because they lose the market incomes and future prospects that come from working, and consequently they are consigned to perpetual poverty and dependency.

The nation's welfare programs also create incentives for family breakup and bearing children out of wedlock. Marriage to a working husband disqualifies a mother for welfare assistance, but having a child out of wedlock qualifies her for extensive welfare assistance. The current welfare system also provides the means to bear children out of wedlock without working. These counterproductive incentives produce poverty, need, dependency, and other pathologies that tend to result (though not invariably) from single parenthood. The tragic truth is that America's trillion-dollar welfare system is the primary cause of poverty in America today.

Social Security and Medicare discourage workers from saving for retirement by providing a free income and free health care without saving. As a result, the economy loses enormous amounts of saving and investment for retirement that would contribute massively to jobs, growing wages, higher economic growth, and prosperity today. When they retire, seniors lose the much higher benefits and accumulations of wealth they would otherwise receive through a lifetime of savings and investment earning market returns.

The health care system – rife with government intrusion at all levels – induces high health care costs through the counterproductive incentives of third-party payment. With the government or an insurance company always paying the bills, patients have no incentives to avoid unnecessary health care costs or to shop for lower-cost health care when that is feasible. Consequently, doctors and hospitals have no incentive to compete to reduce costs to attract patients, because patients are not choosing doctors and hospitals on the basis of costs. The result: high health care costs that lead to more uninsured who can't afford or don't want to pay the accompanying high health insurance premiums.

To add further insult to injury, the higher taxes needed to finance all the tax and redistribution entitlement benefits directly reduce economic growth, prosperity, jobs, and wages even further.

Modernizing the Safety Net

The fundamental breakthrough that must be understood is that modern social safety nets based on modern capital and labor markets with pro-growth market incentives to promote positive rather than self-destructive behaviors would not be a costly burden on the nation's taxpayers. Rather, such properly structured safety nets would be major contributors to America's economic growth and prosperity and, consequently, to the American Dream.

The reforms described in this book would reduce government spending by at least half from what it would be otherwise. If federal spending on our current course is headed toward 80 percent of GDP, these reforms will reduce it by more than three-fourths from that level, to much less than 20 percent of GDP.

Additionally, the poor, retirees, those who need health care, and the disabled would be helped much more by this new, modernized, social safety net. Seniors, for example, would get higher rather than lower retirement benefits and would enjoy better health care than they can get under Medicare today, especially after Obamacare. And by relying on a lifetime of savings and investment, rather than taxpayers, for their benefits, they will be contributing directly to increasing economic growth, prosperity, jobs, and wages for working people today.

Through these reforms we can win the war on poverty after all these years, eliminating involuntary poverty. With the social safety net relying more on modern labor markets to support the poor, private employers would be paying the poor to work and contribute to the economy, instead of taxpayers paying the poor not to work. This is how the first major national entitlement reform, the 1996 welfare reforms, was won on a bipartisan basis, with more than 100 Democrats in Congress voting for it and a Democrat president signing it. Proponents successfully argued those reforms would be better for the poor, which they turned out to be.

Under the reforms proposed in this book, health care for all would be assured, with no individual mandate and no employer mandate. This would not require a government takeover of health care. There would be no denial of health care and no health care rationing by third parties, whether government or insurance companies, as is inevitable under government health care systems such as Obamacare. Costs would be controlled instead by introducing personal market incentives into the health care system, resulting in restored competition among health care providers and insurers.

All of these reform proposals are based on proven reforms that have already worked in the real world, mostly in the United States but also abroad. This is not just ivory-tower theory. We can be confident of the results.

The proposed reforms also are fundamentally based on the concept of individual choice. That makes apparently intractable entitlement and other reforms politically feasible. In regard to personal accounts for Social Security and Medicare, each citizen is offered the choice of the old or the new system. The reform is not imposed on anyone who doesn't want it. But experience and logic show people will overwhelmingly choose the reformed system. After all, choice inherently means increased freedom, which people rightly see as a positive in itself.

Welfare reform is based on cash paid for work, with the poor free to make their own choices from there. Reform of Medicare and Medicaid is based on liberating seniors and the poor to choose private insurance alternatives for their benefits, including health savings accounts, which maximize patient power and choice in health care. Obamacare would be repealed and replaced with full freedom to choose private health insurance as well, with no individual mandate and no employer mandate telling workers and employers what health coverage they must buy.

These are the reasons why the title of this book is "Power to the People."

With the reforms based on individual choice serving the poor, seniors, those who need health care, and the disabled far better for just a fraction of the costs, these entitlement reforms are not just politically *feasible*: They would be politically *popular* as well. These new insights will redraw the political debate. It is no longer the Left offering free handouts covering all the basics and more for everyone, versus the Right meekly calling for cuts in the explosive rate of cost growth. The free market's safety net is far better for the poor, seniors, and those who need health care than the Left's government power safety net of impoverishing over-taxation, over-regulation, and disabling benefits, draining the economy of growth and vitality.

Today, the Left is insisting there be no change to old-fashioned, outdated, financially unsustainable, counterproductive entitlements, whereas free-market innovators of the Right are offering fully modernized safety nets that rely on modern capital and labor markets and positive, pro-growth, market incentives, to better serve the poor, seniors, those who need health care, and the disabled, at just a fraction of the cost of the current programs.

These reforms are the key to enabling the United States to avoid the financial catastrophe of Greece and other European social-welfare states. This is what makes entitlement reform more than politically winnable.

2

Social Security Personal Accounts: Prosperity for All

The baby boom generation already has begun to retire on Social Security and Medicare. For decades now, the federal government's own official reports have been showing Social Security would not be able to pay all benefits promised to the baby boom without dramatic tax increases.

In 2010, Social Security began running a cash deficit for the first time since President Ronald Reagan saved the program from financial collapse in 1983. Under what the government's actuaries call intermediate assumptions, those deficits will continue until 2033, when the combined Social Security trust funds run out of money to pay promised benefits. After that, paying all promised Social Security and Medicare benefits eventually will require almost doubling the current total payroll tax of 15.3 percent to nearly 30 percent.

Under what the government's actuaries call pessimistic assumptions, the Social Security trust funds will run out of money to pay promised benefits by 2029. After that, paying all benefits promised to today's young workers eventually would require raising the total payroll tax rate to 44 percent, three times current levels, and ultimately more.

Personal family savings, investment, and insurance accounts would solve the long-term financing crisis of Social Security and Medicare without benefit cuts or tax increases. They would provide the foundation for restored prosperity for working people for the rest of this century and beyond.

A "Pay as You Go" System

Social Security operates as a pure tax and redistribution system, with no real savings and investment anywhere. Even when the system was running annual surpluses, close to 90 percent of the money coming in was paid out within the year to pay current benefits.

Even the remaining annual surpluses were not saved and invested. They were lent to the federal government and spent on other government programs, from foreign aid to bridges to nowhere, with the Social Security trust funds receiving only internal federal IOUs promising to pay the money back when it is needed to pay benefits.

Those IOUs are rightly accounted for in federal finances not as assets but as part of the Gross Federal Debt, subject to the national debt limit. They do not represent savings and investment but actually additional liabilities of federal taxpayers. As a technical, legal matter, they are nothing more than a statement of the legal authority that Social Security has to draw from general revenues, in addition to payroll taxes.

The Social Security trust funds currently hold about $2.7 trillion in such IOUs. The real problem is not that the government cannot be counted on to pay those IOUs back. The problem is that it's going to be hell – for you – to pay them back.

When Social Security runs a deficit, as it is doing today and will do indefinitely into the future until the trust funds are exhausted, Social Security will turn some of those trust fund IOUs over to the U.S. Treasury to get money back to continue paying promised benefits. But there is no cash or other savings and investment held in reserve to pay back those IOUs. So where does the U.S. Treasury plan to get the money to pay them back? *From you.*

Since those IOUs are national debt, not assets of the federal government, they are owed by you, and you will have to pay them back for retirees to continue to receive all their promised Social Security benefits. Paying back the IOUs will be in addition to the hundreds of billions of dollars you and other taxpayers must pay in payroll taxes each year. When Social Security comes to the Treasury turning in trust fund IOUs to get the cash to pay promised benefits, the Treasury will get that cash either by raising your taxes or by borrowing still more and running even bigger deficits.

This pattern will continue until the Social Security trust funds run out of IOUs, in 2033 under intermediate assumptions.[1] From 2010, when the deficits started, until trust fund exhaustion in 2033, the American people will have to come up with roughly $7.3 trillion to cover all the IOUs in the Social Security trust funds (because the interest "earned" on the trust fund bonds each year is paid with still more IOUs).[2] That is in addition to continuing payroll taxes. Clearly, the Social Security financing crisis has already begun.

The Long-Term Financial Crisis

After 2033, when the Social Security trust funds run out, paying all promised Social Security benefits will require sharp increases in payroll taxes. Under so-called intermediate assumptions, the current total Social Security payroll tax rate of 12.4 percent will have to jump by close to 40 percent to start, to about 17 percent, climbing still further in the following years.[3]

But the Social Security actuaries admit it could be even worse than that. Under so-called pessimistic assumptions, which may be the most realistic, the Social Security trust funds run out in 2029.[4] Paying all promised benefits in 2030 would require raising the total Social Security payroll tax rate from 12.4 percent today to 19 percent, an increase of almost 60 percent.[5] By 2065, when today's young workers will be retiring, paying all promised benefits would require a payroll tax rate of nearly 23 percent, close to double the current rate.[6] Eventually, Social Security payroll taxes would have to grow to 26 percent to pay all promised benefits.[7]

But even this does not account for the whole problem. The Hospital Insurance portion of Medicare, Medicare Part I, is financed by the HI payroll tax, which is currently 2.9 percent of all payroll with no maximum taxable income, split between employer and employee. The HI program is already in deficit, with the trust fund projected to run out of funds to pay promised benefits by 2017. Counting HI along with Social Security, paying all promised benefits by the time today's young workers retire would require raising the total payroll tax rate from 15.3 percent today to 27 percent, on its way eventually to 30 percent, under intermediate assumptions.[8] Under pessimistic assumptions, paying all promised benefits to today's young workers would require raising the payroll tax rate to 44 percent, three times current levels, on its way to 52 percent.[9]

Payroll tax rates in these ranges will cause soaring unemployment, which in turn will mean less revenue than expected, which will require still higher tax rates. This gives a bracing new reality to the term "death spiral."

The root cause of this long-term fiscal disaster is the fundamental structure of Social Security financing. Social Security operates on a "pay-as-you-go" basis. That means the tax money paid by workers today is not saved and invested for their future retirement. The great majority of that money is instead immediately paid out to finance current benefits. The future benefits of today's workers would then be paid not out of the savings and investment of their past tax payments, but out of the future taxes to be paid by future workers when today's workers are retired.

With almost all of the money coming into the program immediately going out to finance current benefits, there is little margin for error when adverse developments threaten the financing balance. With a fully funded savings and investment system, by contrast, a huge accumulation of reserves provides a much greater margin of safety.

Major adverse developments have greatly scrambled Social Security's pay-as-you-go balance. First there was the birth of the baby boom generation after World War II. The fertility rate, or lifetime births per woman, was more than 3.0 by 1947, on its way to a peak of 3.68 in 1957. The rate remained above 3.6 until 1960 and was still 3.3 in 1963.[10] Those born in 1947 are 68 years old in 2015, and over the next 20 years the baby boom generation is going to retire, massively increasing the benefit obligations Social Security must pay.

To make matters worse, this baby boom generation was quickly followed by a baby bust. The new public availability of the birth control pill and swiftly changing social mores in the 1960s caused the nation's demographics to turn on a dime. The fertility rate collapsed to 2.88 in 1965, 2.42 in 1969, and 2.25 in 1971.[11] Just maintaining a stable population requires a fertility rate of 2.1. In 1972 the rate fell to 1.99, down 40 percent in just nine years.[12] The fertility rate continued to decline, reaching a bottom of 1.74 in 1976.[13] It stayed near that level until starting an increase in 1987 toward a level of 2.0 in 1989. It has remained near that level since then.[14]

This fertility double whammy is disastrous for a pay-as-you go system. Just when the huge baby boom generation is retiring and causing benefit expenditures to soar, the generation behind them paying taxes to support those benefits is much smaller than expected, causing a sharp drop in expected tax revenues.

But there is still more. Life expectancy in America has long been booming, which you might expect to be good news for everyone. But not for Social Security. In 1940 life expectancy was 61.4 years for males and 65.7 years for females. Social Security, adopted in 1935 with a retirement age of 65, would not be seen as a great financial burden then. But since then, life expectancy has grown 13.6 years for males, to 75 years, and 14 years for females, to 79.7 years. And of course it is expected to increase even more over the coming decades.

This will make the huge cost of benefits for the baby boom generation so much greater, because they will be living so much longer in retirement. For Social Security today to be an equivalent burden to what it seemed to be in the 1930s, the retirement age would have to be 79, due to the increased life expectancy alone, even before counting the huge increase in numbers of the baby boom generation.

These powerful demographic factors have caused the collapsing number of workers financing each retiree, financial death for a pay-as-you-go system. In 1945, there were 42 workers paying into Social Security for every retiree drawing out benefits.[15] In 1950, there were still 16.5 workers per beneficiary.[16] But the changes in fertility rates starting almost 70 years ago and increased life expectancy have radically revised these ratios. Today there are 3.3 workers per covered beneficiary.[17] By 2032 under the intermediate projections there will be only 2.1, on the way down to 1.9.[18] Under the pessimistic projections, by 2033 there will be 1.9 workers per beneficiary, on the way down to 1.4.[19]

In a pay-as-you-go system, where current workers pay the taxes to support the current retirees directly without investment and accumulating returns, a steep decline in the ratio of taxpayers to beneficiaries means a steep increase in taxes per worker to finance the benefits per retiree. This is reflected in the long-term projections of Social Security finances discussed above.

Why Social Security Is a Bad Deal for Working People

Now let's engage in a fantasy and assume all promised Social Security benefits could somehow be paid. In other words, let's just assume away the entire financial crisis we just discussed. The sad truth is that even if Social Security could somehow pay all the benefits promised under current law, those benefits would represent a poor deal in return for retirees' years of work and tax payments.

To evaluate Social Security, start by taking the actuarial value of all of the program's benefits: retirement benefits, survivors' benefits, and disability benefits. Then compare that to the actuarial value of the program's taxes. An earlier study[20] examined a hypothetical family where the husband works and earns the average income for full-time male workers each year and the wife works and earns the average income for full-time female workers each year. They have two children who each entered the workforce in 1985 at age 22, right after they graduated from college.

Even if all their promised Social Security benefits were somehow paid, those benefits would represent an annual real rate of return of less than 1 percent (0.78 percent) on the taxes paid by these two workers and their employers over their working careers. Almost all hypothetical two-earner couples examined in the study would receive a real return right around this 0.78 percent return. Single workers get an even worse deal. A full-time average-income single worker would receive a real return through the system of 0.31 percent. Overall, for most young workers today, even if the program could somehow pay all of its promised benefits, Social Security would pay a real return of 1.5 percent or less.

Many above-average-income workers would actually receive a negative real return from the system, again even assuming all promised benefits are somehow paid. A negative real return is like depositing your money in the bank, and instead of the bank paying you interest, you pay the bank interest on your deposit. This is what Social Security already is for a lot of people today. There are workers today who along with their employers are paying more than $10,000 a year, each and every year, into Social Security, but instead of getting any real interest on that money at all, they are effectively losing money on it every year with a negative real rate of return from the system. This is counting the value of all promised benefits from the program on an actuarial basis, survivors and disability benefits as well as retirement benefits.

Worst of all, this is where Social Security is heading for all workers in the future. If the government raises taxes or cuts benefits, or does both, to eliminate the long-term deficits of Social Security, then the effective rate of return under Social Security will decline further for all workers. Eventually, virtually all workers under Social Security would be driven down into the range of negative effective real returns.

By contrast, consider standard long-term market returns workers would earn in a savings and investment system. Jeremy Siegel, in his definitive book *Stocks for the Long Run*, documents the real annual compound rate of return on corporate stocks in the United States over the 200-year period

1802 to 2001 was 6.9 percent.[21] It was the same 6.9 percent over the period 1926 to 2001, which included the Great Depression, World War II, the Korean War, the Vietnam War, and the Great Inflation of the 1970s.[22]

From 1926 to 2009, the real rate of return on large-cap stocks, representing the larger companies in America, was 8.64 percent. The real rate of return on small-cap stocks, representing smaller, mid-size firms, was 13.17 percent. A sophisticated, diversified portfolio of 90 percent large-cap and 10 percent small-cap stocks earned a 9.1 percent real return over that period. This period covers the 2008 financial crisis.

Moreover, over the entire postwar era (since 1946) corporate bonds have averaged a real return of 4 percent.[23] Harvard University professor Martin Feldstein, chairman of the National Bureau of Economic Research, and his associate Andrew Samwick calculated in 1997 a portfolio of 60 percent stocks and 40 percent bonds would have generated a real return of 5.5 percent since 1946, and the same return over the period going back to 1926.[24]

Compounding these much higher returns over a lifetime adds up to an enormous difference as compared to the much lower returns offered by Social Security's pay-as-you-go tax and redistribution system. Let's go back to our average-income two-earner couple. Suppose they could save and invest the taxes that would otherwise go into Social Security, in their own family personal account over their entire lives. Suppose funds are set aside each year to buy private life and disability insurance that would pay at least the same survivors and disability benefits as Social Security promises. The rest of their funds are saved and invested each year in a diversified portfolio of half stocks and half bonds earning a conservative real return on average of 5 percent, after paying for all administrative costs to manage the account.

This average-income family would reach retirement with a personal account fund of $1,223,602 in today's dollars, after adjusting for inflation. That fund would be able to pay out of the continuing investment returns alone about twice what Social Security promises to pay them under current law, while still allowing them to leave the $1.2 million fund to their children. Or they could use the fund to buy themselves an annuity that would pay them more than four times what Social Security currently *promises*, let alone what it can pay.

All workers, of all income levels and family combinations, would get much higher benefits saving and investing in the market through personal accounts than the benefits Social Security even promises today, which the program cannot pay. Two low-income spouses earning little more than the minimum wage over their entire careers would reach retirement with well over half-a-million dollars in their personal accounts in today's dollars. That fund would be sufficient to pay them more than three times what Social Security promises but cannot pay.

Just think about the sweeping changes in our society that would result if workers at all income levels were accumulating several hundred thousand dollars in their own personal accounts by retirement. All workers would be accumulating a substantial direct ownership stake in the nation's business and industry. And all workers would consequently prosper along with the American economy. This would be a historic breakthrough in the personal prosperity of working people.

In the 1800s, the Homestead Act opened land ownership to working people. The law said if you got your family out to open land, settled on it in a new home, fenced it in, and worked it to produce crops or raise cattle, the land would be yours. Many people of little means did just that, and they built a family legacy of prosperity that succeeded them in following generations. Land ownership in America became widespread as a result.

In the 1900s, the Federal Housing Administration and later similar agencies opened easy mortgages and homeownership to average-income working people. With a reasonably manageable downpayment and hard, consistent work to make the monthly payments, average- and moderate-income families could own their own homes and prosper along with the rest of the market. Today close to 70 percent of Americans own their own homes.

Now, in 2015, the next great breakthrough in the personal prosperity of working people would be personal accounts for Social Security. Even the lowest-income workers would be able to provide their children with a major financial boost with the substantial funds accumulated in their personal accounts by retirement. As a result, new, private-sector capital would flow into the inner city and other poor communities across the nation. This would provide a financial foundation for higher education, new small businesses, the launching of professional careers, the construction of new housing, and other milestones on the road to prosperity.

Across the United States, new savings and investment would flow through the personal accounts, increasing economic growth. The personal accounts over time would transform the payroll tax into a wealth-building asset owned by families, and this effective tax relief would further spur the economy. The result would be new jobs and higher wages and family income for working people. Feldstein estimates the present value of the future economic gains from shifting from pay-as-you-go Social Security to a fully funded savings and investment system like personal accounts is $10 trillion to $20 trillion.[25]

Why Personal Accounts Work

What explains the enormous gulf between what can be earned through Social Security as compared to private savings and investment? That stems from the fundamental pay-as-you-go financing of Social Security. Because of that financing structure, there is no actual savings and investment at all anywhere in the Social Security system. The great majority of the money paid into Social Security is immediately paid out to finance current benefits. Any money left over is loaned to the federal government and immediately paid out for other government spending, in return for IOUs in the Social Security trust funds. So that money, too, is spent and not saved.

Social Security is not a savings and investment system. It is a tax and redistribution system, where the money is taken from one group of people through taxes and redistributed to other people in benefits and other government spending.

What are the implications of this pay-as-you-go, tax and redistribution financing for Social Security? For one, like any Ponzi scheme, the program was, in fact, a good deal for those who got into it at the beginning. Money was pouring into Social Security with no justified claims on it due to past tax payments. The money was not to be saved and invested for the future benefits of the taxpayers at the time. So the money could be used to pay generous benefits to those just retiring. Those early retirees had paid very little into the program in the past, because it was in effect for only a few years before their retirement. So the benefits they received represented a very high return on whatever they had paid in.

The classic example is the very first Social Security recipient, Ida M. Fuller of Vermont. She and her employer had paid a total of $44 into Social Security before she retired in 1940. She went on to live another 35 years, passing away at age 100 in 1975. During that time she collected close to $20,000 in benefits, an enormous return on an investment of $44.

But over time, workers pay higher and higher taxes for more and more of their working years. As late as 1949, the maximum annual Social

Security tax was still only $60. By 1957, the tax had tripled, but it was still only $189. Twenty years after the Social Security tax had begun, that was all that had to be paid for all of Social Security's promises to each worker. No wonder the program was so popular then.

By 1966, the tax had almost tripled again, to $554. By 1974, it had almost tripled again, to $1,544. By 1980, just six years later, the tax was $3,175. By then the total payroll tax rate was 12.26 percent on the first $25,900 of wages for the year. By 1990, the total payroll tax was 15.3 percent on the first $51,300 of wages, resulting in a maximum tax of $7,848 for the year, close to tripling again from 1980.

For 2007, the payroll tax of 15.3 percent applied to the first $97,500 of wage income, for a total tax of $14,917. But 2.9 percentage points of the tax, the portion that goes to Medicare, applies to all wage income without limit. So even this $14,917 is no longer the maximum tax for the year.

Eventually, the system reaches a point where workers are retiring having paid these high taxes for their entire careers. Then, even the benefits promised to them by the system are not a good deal in return. With no savings and investment in the system, these workers are losing the accumulating and compounding returns that would be earned each year by real savings and investment. They get any return at all from the pay-as-you-go, tax and redistribution system only to the extent that total tax revenues to the system can be raised faster and faster over time. Such a system could never remotely keep up with the market returns that would be earned by a savings and investment system.

The bottom line is that a lifetime of savings and investment would always result in more benefits and personal wealth than a lifetime of no savings and investment, which is all Social Security is.

The full social gain in switching from a purely redistributive pay-as-you-go system like Social Security to a fully funded, real savings and investment system like personal accounts is measured not by the rate of return on stock investments, or by the market returns on various bonds, but by the before-tax real rate of return to capital. Feldstein understood this all the way back in the 1970s, but too many self-satisfied academics have since been lost in confusion over this critical point. The before-tax real rate of return to capital measures the full value of the increased production resulting from increased savings and investment. That is actually higher than long-term stock returns, because those stock returns are partially after-tax returns left after the multiple taxation of capital at the corporate and business level.[26]

Workers can gain the advantages of a savings and investment system through personal accounts without giving up the social safety net provided by Social Security today and exposing workers to excessive risks. There is no reason why workers with personal accounts cannot be provided the same government guarantee as Social Security now provides. As included in the personal accounts bill introduced in Congress discussed below, the government can guarantee that all workers with personal accounts would receive at least as much in benefits as promised by Social Security under current law. This is possible because market capital investment returns are so much higher than what the pay-as-you-go purely redistributive Social Security system can even promise today, let alone what it can pay. Few, if any, workers would have to rely on the safety net, resulting in little cost to taxpayers.

This is especially so since, as discussed further below, workers would be given the opportunity to choose investments for their personal accounts through a structured framework that would be easy for unsophisticated investors. Workers would choose highly diversified investment funds sponsored by experienced private-sector investment fund managers approved and regulated by the federal government for safety and soundness. Average workers would not have to be experts in picking and choosing individual stocks and bonds. They need only choose an investment fund from a list of options approved by government regulators, which would include simple stock index funds with no discretionary investment management. Through this process, the government also would be able to control and limit the risks that could be taken with personal account investments.

With these protections, personal accounts would not actually displace Social Security. Instead they would expand and modernize the Social Security framework to rely on real savings and capital investment rather than counterproductive tax and redistribution. That is the key to transforming Social Security into a prosperity system for working people.

Proven to Work

Chile's Success Story
The best model of a true personal account option for Social Security was adopted in the South American nation of Chile more than 25 years ago.

Chile was the first nation in the Western Hemisphere to adopt a traditional social security system, doing so in 1925, ten years before the United States. But by 1980 Chile's social security system was suffering from many of the problems the U.S. system faces today. Payroll tax rates were 26 percent or higher, yet the system was running large and growing deficits. The promised benefits were inadequate and represented a poor return for the huge tax burden Chileans bore.

To address those problems, Chile adopted a new personal account system that became effective on May 1, 1981. Workers are free to choose the new personal accounts or stay in the old social security system. Those who choose the personal accounts pay, in place of the old social security taxes, 10 percent of their wages each month into a personal account they directly and personally own.

For investment of their account funds, workers choose from among 20 or so alternative investment funds approved and regulated by the government for this purpose.[27] The funds are each managed by an experienced private-sector investment management company, called an AFP (Administradora de Fondos de Pensiones). Among the AFPs are major American financial firms, such as Chase Bank and State Street Global Advisors, and firms affiliated with Chilean labor unions.[28] These companies choose the specific stocks, bonds, and other investments for their funds, creating a highly diversified and sophisticated portfolio subject to government regulation mandating diversification and excluding high-risk investments.

Each investment company is required by law to pay at least a minimum rate of return on the personal account investments, set as a percentage of the average return earned by all 20 AFPs for the year. Workers can change AFPs on short notice. This creates intense competition among the investment firms to provide higher returns and better service.[29]

Workers need not be experienced investors to succeed in the personal account system. They need only to pick one of the 20 investment funds, and the investment company will choose the individual stocks, bonds, and other investments for the worker.

In retirement, workers can use some or all of the funds in their accounts to purchase an annuity from their chosen investment management company or any other financial institution offering such products. The annuity guarantees the worker a specified monthly income for life, indexed to inflation. The annuity also pays a specified survivors benefit for the worker's spouse or other dependents after the worker dies.

Alternatively, the worker can forego any annuity and just take regular withdrawals from the personal account, subject to restrictions based on the life expectancy of the worker and of any dependents eligible for benefits. Any funds remaining in the personal account at death go to the worker's family or other designated heirs.

Workers who were already in the labor force for several years when the reform was adopted and chose the personal accounts were given recognition bonds to be held in their accounts in return for the taxes they already had paid into the old system. The amount of the bonds was set so that with prospective, specified interest they would equal the accrued benefits these workers had earned from their past payments into the old system.

The government in Chile backs the accounts with a guarantee that all workers will get at least a minimum benefit in retirement equal to about 40 percent of average wages. This is about what the U.S. Social Security system pays to average-income workers. If the benefits payable through a Chilean worker's personal account by retirement are not enough to pay at least this minimum benefit, the government provides whatever additional funding is necessary out of general revenues to finance the minimum benefit. *After almost 30 years of experience under this system, the Chilean government never has had to make a payment under this guarantee, including during the recent worldwide financial crisis.*

The investment companies, or AFPs, are entities legally separate from the personal account funds they manage.[30] So if an AFP ever should suffer financial difficulties, there would be no losses to the personal accounts of the workers. If necessary, government regulators would take over an AFP's personal accounts and redistribute them among other AFPs of the workers' choosing. But in 30 years since the Chilean personal account system has been adopted, that has never happened, again even through the recent worldwide financial crisis.[31]

Chilean workers also contribute an additional 2.3 percent of wages for the purchase of group life and disability insurance through their AFP, taking the place of the pre-age-65 survivors and disability benefits of the old system.[32] All of the benefits paid by the new personal account system, including all of the assets in the accounts, are automatically indexed for inflation. This means the chosen investment management companies must pay annual adjustments into the accounts and to the payable benefits to keep everything stable in real terms, after inflation. This reflects history in Chile where the population suffered in the past through brutal bouts of inflation.[33]

Within 18 months of adoption of these Chilean social security reforms, 93 percent of workers chose to switch to the new personal account system. Twenty-five percent did so in just the first month.[34] José Piñera, the Chilean minister of labor at the time who spearheaded the reform, said, "They moved faster than Germans going from East to West after the fall of the Berlin Wall."[35]

By 2004, after 25 years of experience under the reform, the real rate of return on personal account investments in Chile averaged a stunning 10.2 percent.[36] Pensions equal to 70 percent of pre-retirement income, almost twice what U.S. Social Security pays on average, can be financed with a real return of less than half that, at 4 percent, which is what reform advocates had expected.[37] With just half the taxes of the old system, the personal accounts even by 1997 were paying retirees nearly 80 percent of their average income in the last 10 years before retirement.[38] As workers retire having invested in the accounts for more of their careers, their benefits relative to their pre-retirement incomes will rise even further.

Within a few years after the reform was adopted, annual economic growth in Chile reached 7 percent, double the country's historic rate, while unemployment fell to 5 percent.[39] The higher savings and lower taxes resulting from the personal account reforms are recognized as major contributors to that economic growth.[40] After 20 years under the reforms, the savings in the personal accounts totaled 70 percent of GDP.[41] Chile is well on its way to becoming a fully developed First World economy.

Chile's reform has been such a success that seven other nations in Latin America have acted to adopt similar reforms: Peru in 1993, Argentina and Colombia in 1994, Mexico, Bolivia, and El Salvador in 1997, and Uruguay in 1999.[42] The reforms often have been compromised from the original Chilean model, and governments have not always been stellar in implementation. But the result nevertheless has been huge benefits from the essential elements of reform. Similar reforms have flowered in Australia,[43] Great Britain, Hungary, Poland,[44] and elsewhere.[45]

Success in the United States

We don't have to go all over the world to find models for personal accounts. We have a highly successful model right here in the United States.

In 1981, public-sector workers employed by Galveston County, Texas voted to opt out of Social Security into a new, defined-contribution plan under a provision of federal law at the time that allowed state and local government workers to make this choice.[46] In 1982, local government workers in Matagorda and Brazoria counties next door voted to join them.

Under the Galveston plan, 9.737 percent of a worker's salary is contributed to the defined-contribution account each year. The money goes to a bank, First Financial Benefits of Houston, which then lends the money long-term to top-rated financial institutions for a guaranteed interest rate, which has averaged between 7.5 and 8 percent. The financial institutions make their own investments with the funds and use the earnings to pay the guaranteed interest rate. The risk to workers is greatly reduced, as their investment returns do not rise and fall with the stock market. The workers also do not have to make investment decisions; First Financial does that for them.

Just as in Chile, workers in this real savings and investment plan have enjoyed documented benefits two to three times as much as Social Security promises, with higher survivors and disability benefits as well.[47]

U.S. Federal Employees

Finally, there is another example from the United States, the Thrift Savings Plan (TSP) for federal employees.[48] The plan is provided to federal employees in addition to Social Security, not in place of it. But it has been so successful and so popular that it serves as a model for how a real personal account system can work.

TSP has 3.5 million investors with a total of $158 billion in investments. The maximum federal contribution to the account is 5 percent of salary, which would be matched by 5 percent from the worker, for a total of 10 percent. For investment, the workers choose among six fund options with different mixes of investments among stocks and bonds; they can choose to shift among these funds at any time.

At retirement, workers can use some or all of the assets in their accounts to purchase an annuity guaranteeing a specified monthly income for the rest of their lives. With 10 percent of their salaries going into these personal accounts each year, over an entire career at standard market investment returns workers would receive from TSP much more than Social Security even promises, let alone what it can pay.

Clearly, federal employees have developed a good deal for themselves. What about the rest of us?

Personal Accounts and the Financial Crisis

Didn't the financial crisis prove such personal retirement accounts are a bad idea, as President Barack Obama claims?

William G. Shipman, former principal with State Street Global Advisors (perhaps the largest private pension investment management firm in the world), and I conducted a study of the impact of the financial crisis on lifetime savings and investment. The results were published in *The Wall Street Journal* on October 27, 2010.[49]

We examined the case of a hypothetical senior citizen retiring at the end of 2009 at age 66 who had the freedom to choose personal accounts when he entered the workforce in 1965 at the age of 21. Paying into a personal account what he and his employer otherwise would pay into Social Security, the worker took the riskiest possible path, investing his entire portfolio in the stock market for his 45-year working career. How would he have fared in the financial crisis, as compared to Social Security?

We called the hypothetical worker Joe the Plumber. While working, he earned the average income each year for full-time male workers. His wife, Mary, same age, earned the average income each year for women employed full-time. She invested in the same personal account with Joe, an indexed portfolio of 90 percent large-cap stocks and 10 percent small-cap stocks, earning the exact returns reported each year since 1965.

This average-income couple would have reached retirement at the end of 2009 with accumulated account funds, after administrative costs, of $855,175, almost millionaires. Indeed, they were millionaires for a while. But in the financial crisis they lost 37 percent of their account funds the year before they retired.

This hypothetical can be considered a worst-case scenario, as the couple retired just one year after the worst 10-year stock market performance in American history, from 1999 to 2008. Yet their account would be sufficient to pay them about 75 percent more than Social Security even promises them, increased annually for inflation just like Social Security.

The calculations in this hypothetical example are consistent with the real-world versions of personal accounts. Chile's personal account system survived the financial crisis with no bankruptcies in the personal account investment funds. Nothing had to be paid out on the government guarantee backing the accounts: Even through the financial crisis, the lifetime of savings and investment in the accounts provided benefits greatly exceeding what the old system had promised.

In the Galveston plan in the United States, returns on the accounts declined for a couple of years during the financial crisis, but no one lost his or her retirement funds and all participants still enjoyed much higher benefits than they would have under Social Security. The returns have since recovered. Similarly, the personal accounts enjoyed by federal workers in the Thrift Savings Plan suffered declining returns for a couple of years, but the accounts have since recovered those losses, as documented on the TSP website.

Obama suggests it is unwise to support retirement benefits through private-sector savings and investment because such investment entails market risk. Yet despite the financial crisis, every state and local government pension fund, every corporate pension plan, the federal employee retirement plans, and the successful social security reform in Chile – copied by other countries around the world – continue to be based precisely on capital investment to finance the expected retirement benefits.

The hypothetical Joe and Mary discussed above prove Obama wrong. Outside the fever swamps of the far Left, real market savings and investment are universally recognized as the most efficient and only responsible means of providing for future retirement benefits.

Personal accounts as proposed in this book are just an option all workers would be individually free to accept or reject. Anyone who thinks they are too risky need not open such an account. Moreover, those who open such accounts are not required to invest any of their funds in stocks. They can invest in bond funds, precious metals (including gold), real estate funds, even government-guaranteed bonds or other investments. Finally, these personal account proposals keep the Social Security safety net in place, so even in those extreme cases where the government mistakenly trashes the financial markets, as occurred during the 2008–09 financial crisis and the Great Depression (as discussed in Amity Shlaes' brilliant history *The Forgotten Man*[50] and elsewhere), retirees would not be left without sufficient income.

Model Legislation

In 2005, Rep. Paul Ryan (R-WI) and Sen. John Sununu (R-NH) introduced comprehensive legislation providing for such a personal accounts option for the United States, officially scored by the chief actuary of Social Security. The bill provided for no changes of any sort for those already retired or near retirement; they would continue to receive all of their promised Social

Security benefits in full without any change from current law. But workers up to age 55 would be empowered with the freedom to choose to save and invest in the accounts just half the Social Security payroll tax, roughly the employee share of the tax.

Under the Ryan-Sununu bill, workers would choose investments by picking a fund managed by a private investment firm from a list officially approved for this purpose and regulated for safety and soundness. Companies that wanted to offer investment funds on this list would apply to the U.S. Treasury Department for approval of their firms and the particular investment funds they wanted to offer. The investment funds would have to be highly diversified for investment safety, but they could be invested in a broad range of stocks, bonds, and other investments to maximize returns and benefits for workers. The personal account investments would be kept strictly separate from the rest of the company, as is the case in Chile, so any financial troubles the company might experience would have no effect on the personal account investments.

This framework would make investment easy for unsophisticated investors. They would not have to pick specific stocks and bonds. They simply would choose an investment fund, like a mutual fund, managed by experienced, sophisticated, professional investment fund managers, who would choose the stocks, bonds, and other investments and decide when to buy and when to sell each of them. Workers would be free to change the investment fund they have chosen each year. This would be very much like the highly successful investment systems used in Chile, Galveston, and the federal employee Thrift Savings Plan.

Labor unions and social organizations such as NAACP, La Raza, and AARP could team up with investment firms to offer investment funds to their members. This would allow organizations to tailor investment options to the actuarial characteristics of different groups. For example, since African-Americans suffer from lower life expectancy, NAACP might develop annuities that would pay higher benefits because on average their investors will live fewer years in retirement to collect these benefits. Mining unions might develop early-retirement options for their members, who are unlikely to be able to work in the mines into their late sixties.

In retirement, benefits payable from the personal accounts would substitute for a portion of Social Security benefits based on the degree to which workers exercised the account option over their careers and shifted payroll taxes from Social Security to the accounts. Those currently in the workforce who choose the personal accounts would continue to receive a portion of Social Security retirement benefits under the current system based on the past taxes they already have paid into the program, like the recognition bonds under the Chilean system. Workers also would receive the benefits payable through the personal accounts. Social Security pre-retirement survivors and disability benefits would continue to be paid as they are today.

Consider someone in high school today who chooses the personal account option when he enters the workforce. In retirement, benefits from his personal account would substitute for all of the Social Security retirement benefits promised under the current system. With standard long-term market investment returns, he would receive substantially higher benefits than under the current system.

Now consider someone who is 40 when he first exercises the personal account option. In retirement, the benefits from his account would substitute for about half of his Social Security retirement benefits. He would receive all of the benefits payable through the personal account plus about half the benefits promised under current law from the old Social Security framework. Again, with standard long-term market investment returns on the account, the benefits from the personal account would be substantially higher than the proportion of Social Security benefits they replace.

Now consider someone who is 55 when the new system becomes effective. He opts for the personal account during his remaining working years, shifting the employee share of the Social Security tax to his account each year until retirement. His personal account funds would have fewer years to earn and accumulate returns. But that is taken into account in the actuarial formula that determines what proportion of Social Security benefits the personal account benefits would replace. For this older worker, the personal account would replace 10 to 15 percent of his Social Security benefits under current law. The worker would get all the benefits paid by the personal account plus 85 to 90 percent of the Social Security benefits promised under current law.

The option is designed explicitly so all workers will benefit from the higher market investment returns available through personal accounts for their remaining years of work before retirement. As a result, all workers of all ages and all income levels would receive higher benefits through the personal accounts. Workers also would be free to leave any remaining account funds at death to their families.

The Ryan-Sununu bill also would maintain the current Social Security safety net with a government guarantee that all workers with personal accounts would receive through their personal account and continuing Social Security benefits at least as much as promised by Social Security under current law, similar to the guarantee in Chile. If the total benefit for a retiree with a personal account fell below currently promised Social Security benefits, the federal government would send the retiree a check each month to make up the difference.

The guarantee works because market investment returns are so much higher than what Social Security promises, let alone what it can pay. It is highly unlikely that after 45 years or more of real capital market investment, with any short-term market declines averaged out by market rebounds and booms, workers with personal accounts would end up with less than what Social Security promises.

In other words, it is very unlikely, if not impossible, that a lifetime of savings and investment would add up to less than a lifetime of no savings and investment, which is Social Security as we know it today. It is thus highly unlikely that the guarantee would result in significant costs to taxpayers when the worker retires.

This is all the more true because of the carefully structured investment system described above, with workers choosing among professionally managed investment funds approved and regulated for this purpose. The government can fully limit and control the risks workers are allowed to take with their personal accounts. Such a system has worked well in a range of other contexts, with no losses or need for bailouts after decades of operation.

Workers would be completely free to choose to stay in Social Security without exercising the personal account option at all. There would be no benefit cuts or tax increases for these workers. They would continue to get all the benefits promised by Social Security under current law. This works because, as the chief actuary of Social Security concluded (discussed further below), the personal accounts would be such a good deal that over time all workers would choose them. This in turn would eliminate the long-term deficits of Social Security without benefit cuts or tax increases, as also discussed further below.

By maintaining the current safety net with a federal guarantee and a structure for investment options and benefit payments, the Ryan-Sununu proposal actually expands the current Social Security framework so workers can gain the enormous advantages of market savings and investment.

Another virtue of personal accounts is that workers who finance their own benefits through their own savings and investment can be free to choose their own retirement age. They would have market incentives to choose to delay their own retirement as long as possible, because the longer they wait the more they would accumulate in their accounts and the higher the benefits those accounts could pay.

As a result, millions of workers with less physically taxing jobs would choose on their own to delay their retirement well into their seventies, a result that could never be imposed politically. Other workers whose jobs required heavy physical labor or who for other reasons could not work past their early sixties could retire then. With planning, they or their employers could make additional contributions to the accounts over the years to finance more benefits for that earlier retirement. This is a far superior way to set a retirement age than having politicians impose a one-size-fits-none retirement age.

The Chief Actuary's Score

The chief actuary of Social Security analyzed the Ryan-Sununu bill and published a comprehensive official score estimating its effects. That score is available on the official website of the Social Security Administration.[51]

First, the chief actuary found the personal accounts in the Ryan-Sununu bill would achieve full solvency for Social Security, completely eliminating Social Security deficits over time without any benefit cuts or tax increases. The chief actuary stated, "the Social Security program would be expected to be solvent and to meet its benefit obligations throughout the long-range period 2003 through 2077 and beyond."[52] This results because so much of Social Security's benefit obligations are ultimately shifted to the personal accounts, while the employer share of the tax remains in place.

Over several decades virtually 100 percent of Social Security retirement benefits would be shifted to the personal accounts, as the chief actuary concluded the accounts proposed by Ryan-Sununu would be so beneficial for workers that all would eventually choose them, a conclusion validated by the experience in Chile. That would mean the largest reduction in government spending in world history, as Social Security retirement benefits would be shifted to the private sector. The resulting surpluses are so large they would eliminate the long-term deficits of the disability insurance program as well, even though the reform plan does not otherwise provide for any changes in that program.

The accounts achieve this with no benefit cuts or tax increases. At standard long-term market investment returns, the accounts would produce substantially more in benefits for working people across the board than Social Security now promises, let alone what it can pay. The Ryan-Sununu bill would allow workers to put only half the total Social Security payroll tax into the accounts – but private market investment is so productive that with only half as much paid in, workers still would get much better benefits, as has been true in Chile.

Ryan-Sununu also would eliminate the unfunded liabilities of Social Security, currently officially estimated at $15.1 trillion. This results because over time, pay-as-you-go, non-invested, purely redistributive Social Security is transformed into the fully funded savings- and investment-based personal accounts. This would be the largest reduction in government debt in world history.

Workers would own and control the funds in the personal accounts, just as they do the funds in their IRAs or 401(k)s. After the first 15 years with the Ryan-Sununu personal accounts, workers would have accumulated $7.8 trillion in today's dollars, after adjusting for inflation, according to the chief actuary's score. This is as large as the entire mutual fund industry today. After the first 25 years, workers would have accumulated $16 trillion, again in today's dollars.

Workers would be free to choose to leave some portion of these funds to their families at death. What a boost that would be to future generations, to have such a foundation for their own future prosperity. Imagine a future economy with low-, moderate-, and middle-income families leaving some substantial portion of these accounts to their children, along with a home of substantial value. That would be a financial foundation for higher education, or starting a new small business or a professional practice, or pursuing some other dream.

With such personal accounts, working people at all income levels would hold a substantial ownership stake in the nation's businesses and industries. No other reform would do so much to promote equality of wealth among the American people. According to Feldstein, if Social Security were shifted to a fully funded system like personal accounts, the concentration of real wealth in the United States would be reduced by half.[53]

Other approaches to such equality are based on redistribution punishing the successful, creating counterproductive incentives that drag down the economy. Personal accounts, by contrast, achieve more equality by creating vast realms of new wealth broadly owned throughout the population. This reinforces and strengthens the economy, expanding economic growth.

The personal accounts funnel new rivers of savings and investment into the economy. Higher savings and capital investment mean higher productivity and increased wages for working people. That creates new jobs and new opportunities. The bottom line is increased economic growth. Such increased capital would finance the practical implementation of our rapidly advancing science, leapfrogging our economy further generations ahead. These would be immediate benefits for working people as soon as the plan was adopted.

Moreover, when workers start paying the employee share of the payroll tax into personal accounts they own and control in order to finance their own future benefits, then as a matter of economics that portion of the payroll tax is no longer a tax. The workers are no longer paying that money to the government to finance the benefits of others. They are keeping that money as their own property, and all accumulated investment returns are theirs as well. Through the personal accounts, the payroll tax – the biggest tax most people pay – is transformed into a personal wealth engine for workers and their families.

This has virtually the same positive effect on the economy as eliminating the employee share of the payroll tax. It would cause wages, employment, and overall economic growth to expand more rapidly. A booming economy in which to work is another enormous benefit for working people. This is what happened in Chile, moving from Third World country to the First World.

An Alternative Approach

Instead of financing contributions to the personal accounts from Social Security payroll taxes, with general revenues paid into Social Security to maintain continued payment of current Social Security benefits, as Ryan-Sununu proposed, the personal account contribution could be financed out of general revenues directly, with no reduction in the payroll tax revenues flowing into Social Security. That would avoid AARP's chief past criticism of personal accounts, that they would divert the payroll tax revenues needed to pay today's benefits.[54]

In this scenario, the maximum account contribution could start at half the amount of the employee payroll tax. For workers who exercise that option for their entire careers, the accounts would finance half of their retirement benefits, with the other half coming from the current Social Security system. Those who exercise the option for fewer years would finance proportionally less of their future retirement benefits through the accounts.

This proposal also was scored by the chief actuary of Social Security as sufficient to eliminate the long-term deficits of Social Security through the personal accounts alone, with no benefit cuts and no tax increases.

Ultimately, as workers retire in the future relying on the personal accounts instead of the government to finance half of their retirement benefits, enormous surpluses will be created in Social Security as the payroll tax remains fully in place under this alternative. Under current law, those surpluses would flow back into general revenues, eventually providing enough funding to cover all future personal account contributions from general revenues.

This alternative would provide all the advantages of Ryan-Sununu, but half as much, until the option was expanded to the full employee share of the payroll tax.

Financing the Transition
Any plan for personal accounts for Social Security involves a transition financing issue. As discussed above, Social Security currently operates on a pay-as-you-go basis; almost all of the money that comes in goes out immediately to pay current benefits. If part of the money coming in goes for savings and investment in personal accounts instead, additional funds will have to come from somewhere else to continue paying all benefits promised to today's retirees. If the accounts are financed from general revenues as under the alternative approach, those general revenues have to be financed as well. The need for this transition financing phases out over time as workers relying on their personal accounts instead of payroll taxes retire.

This is a cash-flow financing issue, however, not a matter of transition "costs." What the transition is financing is the increased savings and investment involved in shifting from a pay-as-you-go system with no real savings and investment to a fully funded savings- and investment-based system.

Consider this: When you save $1,000 in a bank, you don't think that doing so cost you $1,000. It doesn't cost you anything, because you still have the money, in your savings account. Of course, you can't have your cake and eat it too: You can't spend the $1,000 you are saving, or else you wouldn't be saving it. That may create a cash-flow problem for you, depending on the state of your personal finances. But it is not a matter of the savings costing you $1,000.

The transition financing for a system of personal retirement accounts is thus a matter of effectively financing the savings going into the personal accounts of working people across the United States, ultimately amounting to trillions of dollars. That accumulated savings and investment is not a cost to the economy; it is a mighty, productive contributor to the economy. The working people seeing money growing in their own personal accounts would certainly recognize it is not a cost but in fact an asset. The personal accounts are just a politically sophisticated means of shifting from the current, completely non-invested, Social Security system to a fully funded system based entirely on private savings and investment. That shift should be readily recognized as the complete, responsible, and desirable solution to the problems of Social Security.

This transition financing can be covered by the reduced government spending resulting from other entitlement reforms that will be discussed in later chapters of this book. With the transition financed entirely by reduced spending, the personal accounts would contribute to national savings and investment with no offset for increased government borrowing.

The workability of this approach was demonstrated by the Ryan Roadmap,[55] the comprehensive legislation introduced in 2010 by Paul Ryan (R-WI), at the time chairman of the House Budget Committee and now chairman of the House Ways and Means Committee. That proposal included personal accounts for Social Security, fundamental reform of Medicare and Medicaid, general health care reform, tax reform, and other budget reforms. The Congressional Budget Office (CBO) officially scored the Ryan Roadmap as achieving full solvency for Social Security and Medicare while balancing the federal budget indefinitely into the future, completely eliminating all long-term federal deficits, with no tax increases. The transition to personal accounts for Social Security was fully paid for, effectively by the spending reductions.

A Vision for Reform

Reform of Social Security should begin with legislation along the lines of the Ryan-Sununu bill.

After the initial reform, the personal account option could be expanded to allow substitution of private life insurance for Social Security survivors benefits and private disability insurance for Social Security disability benefits. This could be accomplished with another 2.3 percent of wages, as in Chile, coming out of the employer share of the tax. Eventually, the accounts could be expanded to cover the payroll taxes for Medicare, another 2.9 percent of wages, with the saved funds financing monthly annuity benefits used to purchase private health insurance in retirement, as will be discussed in Chapter 3. The personal accounts would then cover all benefits paid by the payroll tax, but for 11.4 percent of wages, about one-fourth less than the current 15.3 percent payroll tax. After a lifetime of savings and investment of those funds, the benefits would be substantially higher than what Social Security even promises, let alone what it could pay.

With the personal accounts paying for all of the benefits currently financed by the payroll tax, that tax – the biggest burden on working people – would eventually be phased out altogether. Workers instead would be paying into the family wealth engine of their own personal savings, investment, and insurance accounts. This would establish a new foundation of prosperity for working people in America.

In the process, over a period of decades, government spending equivalent to about 10 percent of GDP would be transferred to the private sector, the largest reduction in government spending in world history.

The fatal fallacy persists that it would be politically easier to cut benefits than to enact structural reforms such as personal accounts. For all of the reasons discussed above, a populist, grassroots alliance can be generated to support personal accounts, the only Social Security reform idea ever to show support by large majorities in public opinion polls.

The alternative is to cut a deal with the Washington establishment that will slash Social Security returns and benefits for working people, at the price of agreeing to a tax increase for "balance." This would be economically crippling for the nation and politically crippling for those involved in any such grand bargain.

How Bush Lost Personal Accounts

When George W. Bush ran for president in 2000, he explicitly campaigned on empowering workers with the freedom to choose personal accounts for Social Security. His campaign employed all the positive, populist themes originally envisioned for the reform effort. He emphasized the personal ownership and control workers would enjoy through the accounts, the better returns on investment and consequently higher benefits, the accumulated family funds that could be left as an inheritance to children or other heirs, and the full solvency for Social Security that would be achieved without raising taxes or cutting benefits. He specifically contrasted personal accounts with the unpopular alternatives of raising taxes or cutting benefits. He explained that with the personal accounts, he was modernizing Social Security for a better future.[56] In a major address on Social Security in Rancho Cucamonga, California on May 15, 2000, Bush said,

> Personal accounts build on the promise of Social Security – they strengthen it, making it more valuable for young workers. Senator Moynihan, Democrat, says that personal accounts take the system to its "logical completion." They give people the security of ownership. They allow even low-income workers to build wealth, which they will use for their own retirement and pass on to their children.
>
> Senator [Bob] Kerrey, also a Democrat, recently said: "It's very important, especially for those of us who have already accumulated wealth, to write laws to enable other people to accumulate it, and arrive where we are." Ownership in our society should not be an exclusive club. Independence should not be a gated community. Everyone should be a part-owner in the American Dream.
>
> Yet, without reform, younger workers face a great risk – a lifetime of paying taxes for benefits they may never receive. The reforms I have in mind will actually increase their retirement income.
>
> Within the framework of these principles, we can keep Social Security strong and stable. We can keep our commitments. We can avoid tax increases. And millions of Americans will have an asset to call their own. This is the best thing about personal accounts. They are not just a program, they are your property. And no politician can take them away.[57]

Regarding possible payroll tax increases, Bush added, "Third, the payroll tax must not be raised. We cannot tax our way to reform."[58]

On September 18, 2000, the Cato Institute reported on how candidate Bush was doing with his Social Security personal accounts proposal, saying:

> Social Security has traditionally been a Democratic strong suit but not this year. Whereas polls in the past showed Democrats with a 20-point or more advantage on the question of which party would best handle Social Security, now the parties are running close to even. More important, when voters are asked whether they support Bush's proposal to allow workers to divert a portion of their Social Security taxes to individually owned, privately invested accounts, they strongly endorse the proposal. In the latest Washington Post-ABC News Poll, 59% of voters supported the Bush proposal; 37% were opposed. Vital swing voters are even more supportive of individual accounts. According to a Zogby International poll, 72% of independent voters support individual accounts[59]

In other words, Bush's positive, populist approach of focusing on the personal accounts alone and emphasizing all of their benefits for the common man was working. Cato also applauded Bush's strategy of contrasting the personal accounts with the unpopular alternatives of cutting benefits and raising taxes, saying:

> It was Bill Clinton who best explained the options available to fix Social Security. There are only three: raise taxes, cut benefits, or increase the rate of return by investing Social Security funds. Clinton proposed to do the latter by allowing the government to invest a portion of the Social Security Trust Fund, a dangerous idea that has wisely not seen the light of day. George Bush proposes to do it by allowing workers to invest for themselves. Al Gore rejects both approaches, opposing any investment of Social Security funds. With investment and higher returns off the table, that leaves Gore with only two alternatives; either he raises taxes or cuts benefits. Bush should simply turn to Gore in debate and ask him which of those he plans to do.[60]

Larry Kudlow, a senior official in the Reagan administration, commented in *National Review Online* about the brilliance and effectiveness of Bush's campaign for personal accounts in 2000. Kudlow noted in particular the focus on personal accounts and all of their advantages, in contrast to benefit cuts:

> Way back in time, during the early months of the Reagan Administration, a number of the Gipper's more libertarian economic advisers wanted to trash the New Deal – especially Social Security – by severely rolling back benefits in order to shrink government and curb the budget deficit. Wisely, President Reagan always rejected this approach. Time and again, he reminded his staff that he himself voted for FDR four times and went on to vote for Truman. Throughout the budget arguments, Reagan insisted on invoking and preserving the so-called social safety net.
>
> Yes, he intended to radically transform the economic landscape by slashing marginal tax rates and putting an end to double-digit inflation. And yes, he worked hard to slow domestic spending. But he steadfastly refused to rip large holes through the New Deal/ Great Society safety net, believing that these programs were an integral part of the fabric of American life. What's so interesting to me about George W. Bush's freshly minted Social Security reform plan that provides for individual-retirement-account-investing in the stock market – set forth in a speech today in California – is that he makes it clear that he intends to strengthen and save Social Security, not to destroy it. This is smart Reagan-style politics. ...
>
> Give him credit. Enormous credit. This is 21st Century breakthrough stuff.[61]

Perhaps even more surprising than Bush's politically aggressive, trailblazing embrace of personal accounts for Social Security during the 2000 campaign was what we didn't hear from his opponent in that race, Vice President Al Gore. The way the Washington establishment talks about the current Social Security system in such hallowed terms, you might have expected Gore to pound away at Bush on this issue in massive ad campaigns and through other means.

But Gore didn't. He did criticize Bush, and there were some ads against the personal accounts, especially late in the campaign. But Gore never came close to developing his attack into a major issue of the campaign. The Democrats saw in their own internal polls what Bush already knew: Freedom to choose personal accounts for at least part of Social Security was a very popular, even populist, idea at the grassroots. Polls at the time were consistently showing 60 percent to 70 percent of the public supported personal accounts.

Moreover, strong majorities of base Democrat constituencies – African-Americans, Hispanics, blue-collar workers – supported the idea. Those constituencies viewed personal accounts as their only real chance to start accumulating some personal and family wealth.

Attacking Bush over the issue would at best spread the word that Bush was for the popular accounts. At worst, it would identify Gore as being on the wrong side of the issue. Gore spent more time on a watered down, me-tooism than in attacking Bush on personal accounts. Gore proposed an add-on account on top of Social Security, where workers could save and invest additional money on top of what they pay into Social Security. But many Democrat core voters do not have the discretionary funds for substantial savings on top of Social Security. Moreover, we already have a lot of add-on accounts on top of Social Security, such as IRAs and 401(k)s.

Bush, of course, went on to a narrow victory in 2000, with many saying personal accounts provided a net gain for him. The proposal did not stop him from winning the senior vote in Florida, and without that he would not have been president.

But Bush was not the only candidate who won on personal accounts. In the late 1990s, congressional Republican candidates started running on the idea as part of their platforms. They consistently won. The big breakthrough came in 2002, when the Democrats tried to make personal accounts a pivotal issue in the midterm congressional elections. Top pollster John Zogby summed up the results as follows: "In every campaign where personal accounts were a major issue, the candidate in favor of personal accounts won, and the candidate opposing them lost."

All of these candidates campaigned for personal accounts the way Bush did. They emphasized that the accounts provided a better deal for workers; that benefits for future retirees would go up, not down; that Social Security would be strengthened; and that there would be no tax increases. They did not say they would cut future promised retirement benefits by monkeying with the basic Social Security benefit formula (a proposal called "price-indexing" we will see more of below), delaying the retirement age, raising the cap on the maximum taxable income for Social Security, or otherwise increasing payroll taxes.

In 2004, Bush pledged again to adopt personal accounts for Social Security as a top priority for his second term. His opponent, John Kerry, was even quieter about it than Gore had been. He talked at times about add-on accounts. If Kerry's internal polls had shown Bush was vulnerable over personal accounts, Kerry and the Democrats would have ripped his throat out over it. But again the dog did not bark.

At the start of 2005, Bush had just decisively won reelection while advocating personal accounts for Social Security. Strong polling majorities favored the idea. The Republicans had substantial majorities in both houses of Congress, including 55 senators. Comprehensive personal account legislation had been introduced in both the House and the Senate. And the chief actuary of Social Security had scored that legislation as achieving full solvency for Social Security.

Everything was poised for fundamental, sweeping, historic Social Security reform through personal accounts. But it never happened.

Bush's White House staff in charge of the Social Security reform effort never understood the politics or policy of personal accounts, and they proved uneducable on the subject. They were stuck inside the Washington Establishment box that insisted Social Security reform was all about some combination of tax increases and benefit cuts. In deference to the president's campaign proposals, they lumped personal accounts on top of their tax increase/benefit cut conception of what Social Security reform was all about.

By 2005 there was little evidence of the trailblazing, populist themes and rhetoric the president had so successfully used in arguing for personal accounts during his 2000 campaign in particular. Gone was the discussion of a better deal and better benefits from personal accounts. We heard little about ownership, building personal wealth, and leaving an inheritance to children and family.

Instead, the focus of discussion had moved to a huge cut in future promised Social Security benefits under the label of "price-indexing." As for tax increases, while the president proclaimed during the campaign that "no tax increases" was one of his seven principles of reform and that we could not "tax our way to reform," tax increases were now "on the table."

The mantra came to be that "everything was on the table" – every brutally unpopular idea, such as delaying the retirement age or adding means-testing, along with the one politically successful and transforming idea of personal accounts. The positives of personal accounts were lost in the high weeds of public policy debate. Were benefits going to rise under personal accounts, or fall under price indexing? The public was at best confused.

Under the new White House conception of Social Security reform, personal accounts were the "dessert" to make palatable the "spinach" of benefit reductions.[62] Even White House criticism of those calling for tax increases was short-circuited. The president had been turned away from the positive, personal empowerment approach of the 2000 campaign, which had proven so successful in transforming Social Security from the third rail of American politics to a populist issue on which Republican after Republican was winning elections.

The White House Social Security policy team convinced Bush and senior White House staff that congressional Democrat support for Social Security reform including personal accounts would be won if the president would just publicly announce support for the notion of "price indexing" as well. Price indexing involves changing the fundamental Social Security benefit formula for calculating the future benefits workers would receive at retirement. (Price indexing does not affect the post-retirement Social Security cost of living adjustment.) Instead of growing over time with *wages*, which keeps Social Security benefits stable as a percentage of pre-retirement income, under price indexing the benefits to be paid at retirement grow during the worker's career with *prices*. Since prices grow more slowly than wages each year, price indexing would reduce Social Security benefits over time from currently promised levels, about a 40 percent cut in the future benefits Social Security would pay under current law for today's young workers.

This proposal was directly contrary to the natural political appeal of personal accounts to young workers. It also begged for a response from liberals that tax increases would have to be included in any reform package if benefits were cut.

With personal accounts, such price-indexing was completely unnecessary, as workers over time would be replacing the promised wage-indexed benefits, which Social Security admittedly cannot finance, with the fully funded personal account benefits financed by real savings and investment. But the White House Social Security policy team was impenetrable on this point.

In the fall of 2005, the president himself endorsed price indexing on national television in a highly confusing and forgettable appearance. The public had no idea what he was talking about. The response from congressional Democrats was crickets chirping. Despite White House staff fantasies, not one elected Democrat rose to endorse personal accounts in return for the president's support of price indexing. Indeed, not one elected Democrat rose to endorse price-indexing in any form. How could anyone have expected Democrats to support personal accounts in return for a 40 percent cut in future promised Social Security benefits?

No wonder the more Bush talked about Social Security reform and personal accounts, the more his support dropped on the issue. By the time the president was done trying to promote Social Security reform in late 2005, the polls still showed 50 percent to 60 percent of the public supported personal accounts, down only about 10 points. But when asked if they supported "the president's plan" on Social Security, the public's support dropped by half, to the range of 25 percent to 30 percent. This was the direct result of efforts by the White House Social Security policy staff to shift Social Security reform from the positive, populist model focusing entirely on personal accounts that the president originally supported, to a Pain Caucus model focusing on a package of benefit cuts and tax increases with personal accounts as dessert.

The legacy of sweeping, fundamental Social Security reform would belong to some future president.

Conclusion

Fully funding future retirement benefits through real savings and investment is the only real solution for Social Security and Medicare, eliminating unfunded liabilities entirely. That is what personal accounts do.

We readily understand this when discussing underfunded state and local public employee pension systems and their unfunded liabilities. But somehow when it comes to Social Security and Medicare, with unfunded liabilities that dwarf those of state and local pensions, we suspend reason and ignore what we apply to all other retirement systems.

Shifting to personal accounts for Social Security would result in several breakthroughs:

- Retirement benefits would be paid through the private sector rather than the government, resulting in the greatest reduction in government spending in world history.

- In replacing the Social Security payroll tax with a personal family wealth engine, personal accounts would involve the greatest reduction in taxes in world history.

- The long-term financing crisis of Social Security would be solved, without benefit cuts or tax increases. Working Americans would accumulate hundreds of thousands of dollars in real family wealth over their careers, receiving much higher benefits in retirement than Social Security even promises, let alone what it can pay.

- Americans would choose their own retirement age, instead of having a one-size-fits-no-one retirement age foisted on them by government.

- Social Security would be transformed from a pay-as-you-go system supported by IOUs with no savings and investment, into a fully funded retirement system relying entirely on real savings and investment, resulting in the greatest reduction in effective government debt in world history.

- Working people in the United States would all be capitalists as well as laborers, directly and personally owning the nation's business and industry. This massive, broadly owned savings and investment would do more to increase equality of wealth than any other initiative in world history – not by the redistribution of existing wealth, but through the creation of new wealth, broadly and widely owned.

- Mighty rivers of savings and capital investment would flow into the economy immediately, increasing economic growth, jobs, wages, and income for working people today. Personal accounts would provide the foundation for restored prosperity for working people for the rest of this century and beyond.

Notes

1. 2013 Annual Report of the Board of Trustees of the Old Age and Survivors Insurance and Disability Insurance Trust Funds, May 31, 2013, Table IV.B3.

2. Calculated from 2012 Trustees Report, Table VI.F8.

3. 2013 Trustees Report, *supra* note 1, Table VI.F.2.

4. *Ibid.*, Table IV.B3

5. *Ibid.*, Table IV.B1

6. *Ibid.*

7. *Ibid.*

8. *Ibid.*, Table VI.F2.

9. *Ibid.*

10. *Ibid.*, Table V.A1.

11. *Ibid.*

12. *Ibid.*

13. *Ibid.*

14. *Ibid.*

15. *Ibid.*, Table IV.B2.

16. *Ibid.*

17. *Ibid.*

18. *Ibid.*

19. *Ibid.*

20. Peter J. Ferrara and Michael Tanner, *A New Deal for Social Security* (Washington, DC: Cato Institute, 1998), Chapter 4.

21. Jeremy Siegel, *Stocks for the Long Run* (New York, NY: McGraw-Hill, 2002), 3rd ed.

22. *Ibid.*; *Stocks, Bonds, Bills, and Inflation 2007 Yearbook* (Chicago, IL: Ibbotson Associates).; Jeremy Siegel, *Stocks for the Long Run* (Chicago, IL: Irwin Professional Publishing, 1994).

23. Edgar K. Browning, "The Anatomy of Social Security and Medicare," *The Independent Review*, Vol. XIII, no. 1, Summer 2008, p. 12. See also, Jeremy Siegel, *supra* note 21 (the average real return on corporate bonds over the 200-year period from 1802 to 2001 was 5 percent); José Piñera, "Toward a World of Worker Capitalists," Transform the Americas, www.transformamericas.com, April 2000.

24. Martin Feldstein and Andrew Samwick, "The Economics of Prefunding Social Security and Medicare Benefits," National Bureau of Economic Research *Working Paper* no. 6055, National Bureau of Economic Research, June 1997.

25. Martin Feldstein, "The Missing Piece in Policy Analysis," *American Economic Review*, Vol. 86, no. 2 (May 1996): p. 12. I consider that a conservative underestimate because of the likely effects of combining booming capital investment with rapidly advancing modern technology.

26. *Ibid.*

27. José Piñera, "The Success of Chile's Privatized Social Security," *Cato Policy Report*, Vol. XVIII, Number 4, Cato Institute, August 1995.

28. José Piñera, "Empowering Workers: The Privatization of Social Security in Chile," *Cato Journal* 15, nos. 2–3 (1997).

29. José Piñera, *supra* note 27.

30. *Ibid.*

31. *Ibid.*

32. "The AFP System Myths and Realities," Chilean AFP Association, August 2004, p. 3.

33. This is possible with market investments because inflation is reflected over time in higher capital returns, maintaining stable real returns over the long run. The Chilean system has worked this way successfully for 30 years.

34. José Piñera, *supra* note 28; José Piñera, "Retiring in Chile," Transform the Americas, www.transformamericas.org, 2001.

35. José Piñera, *supra* note 27.

36. Chilean AFP Association, *supra* note 32, p. 4.

37. José Piñera, "Retiring in Chile," *supra* note 34.

38. José Piñera, *supra* note 28; José Piñera, "Toward a World of Worker Capitalists," Transform the Americas, www.transformamericas.com, April 2000.

39. *Ibid.*

40. *Ibid.*

41. José Piñera, "Retiring in Chile," *supra* note 34.

42. José Piñera, "Empowering Workers," *supra* note 28; José Piñera, "Toward a World of Worker Capitalists," *supra* note 38.

43. *Ibid.*

44. *Ibid.*

45. The World Bank, *Averting the Old-Age Crisis* (Oxford: Oxford University Press, 1994); Peter J. Ferrara and Michael Tanner, *A New Deal for Social Security* (Washington, DC: Cato Institute, 1998), Chapter 1: The Worldwide Revolution in Social Security, pp. 1–11.

46. The opt-out provision for public employees was repealed in 1983 because an increasing number of state and local government units were deciding they could provide their employees with a better deal than Social Security, and the federal government did not want to lose so many taxpayers.

47. Testimony of Don Kibbedeaux before the Senate Committee on Finance, Subcommittee on Securities, April 30, 1996; Merrill Mathews, "No Risky Scheme: Retirement Savings Accounts That Are Personal and Safe," Institute for Policy Innovation, *Policy Report* No. 163, January 2002.

48. See https://www.tsp.gov/index.shtml.

49. William G. Shipman and Peter Ferrara, "Private Social Security Accounts: Still a Good Idea," *The Wall Street Journal*, October 27, 2010, p. A17.

50. Amity Shlaes, *The Forgotten Man, A New History of the Great Depression* (New York, NY: Harper Collins, 2007).

51. Steve Goss, chief actuary, Social Security Administration, Estimated Financial Effects of the "Social Security Personal Savings Guarantee and Prosperity Act of 2005" introduced as H.R. 1776 by Representative Paul Ryan and as S. 857 by Senator John Sununu, April 20, 2005, http://www.socialsecurity.gov/OACT/solvency/.

52. Office of the Chief Actuary, Social Security Administration, Estimated Financial Effects of the "Social Security Personal Savings and Prosperity Act of 2004," July 19, 2004.

53. Martin Feldstein, "Social Security and the Distribution of Wealth," *Journal of the American Statistical Association* (December 1976): 90–93.

54. It is interesting to note AARP never raised any concern about President Barack Obama's temporary payroll tax cuts replaced with general revenues for Social Security.

55. Paul Ryan, *Roadmap for America's Future Act of 2010* (H.R. 4529), 111th Congress, September 1, 2010, http://www.roadmap.republicans.budget.house.gov/UploadedFiles/Roadmap2Final2.pdf.

56. "George W. Bush 2000 on the Issues: Social Security," 4President.us, www.4president.us, January 15, 2008; Gov. George W. Bush, "Saving Social Security and Medicare," May 15, 2000 (campaign fact sheet).

57. George W. Bush, Address to the Rancho Cucamonga Senior Citizen Center, Rancho Cucamonga, California, May 15, 2000, pp. 3–5.

58. *Ibid.*, p. 3.

59. Michael Tanner, Memo to George W. Bush: Social Security Is a Winning Issue, September 19, 2000, www.socialsecurity.org.

60. *Ibid.*

61. Larry Kudlow. "W.'s Muscular Social Security Plan: This is 21st Century Breakthrough Stuff," *National Review Online*, May 15, 2000.

62. Jackie Calmes, "Architect of Social Security Plan Perseveres," *The Wall Street Journal*, April 22, 2005.

3

A Better Medicare for Seniors and Taxpayers

During the 2012 election campaigns, Democratic National Committee Chairwoman Debbie Wasserman Schultz described the Medicare reforms proposed by House Budget Committee Chairman Paul Ryan (R-WI) in his 2012 and 2013 House Republican budgets as "literally a death trap for seniors." White House spokesman Jay Carney less dramatically told reporters in 2012 that Ryan's reforms would "change Medicare as we know it."

But it was the Patient Protection and Affordable Care Act (PPACA), commonly known as Obamacare, that already had changed Medicare as we know it. Obamacare cut Medicare by $716 billion over the next 10 years alone, mostly by slashing payments to doctors and hospitals, as the Congressional Budget Office (CBO) and Medicare's own actuaries have documented.[1]

During the 2012 campaign, President Barack Obama and his staff repeatedly said Obamacare did not cut Medicare benefits at all. During a presidential debate, Obama said the $716 billion in Medicare cuts involved only cuts in "overpayments" to doctors and hospitals providing health care to seniors, and to insurance companies that millions of seniors had chosen to provide their Medicare benefits under Medicare Part C. But Medicare "benefits were not affected at all,"[2] the president claimed.

Obama campaign spokeswoman Stephanie Cutter said none of the $716 billion in CBO-documented Obamacare cuts to Medicare involved any cut in Medicare benefits, "not by one dime."[3] It all involved cutting "waste, fraud, and abuse" and "subsidies" in payments to doctors, hospitals, and

47

insurance companies that were providing health care and health insurance coverage to seniors, as chosen by seniors.

Just Send Us the Bill, and We Won't Pay You

But the Medicare actuaries said something different. Medicare Chief Actuary Rick Foster said as a result of the Obamacare cuts, ultimately Medicare payment rates to doctors and hospitals will be one-third what is paid by private insurance and only half what is paid by Medicaid.[4]

Medicaid payment rates are so low, just a fraction of actual costs, that the poor on Medicaid suffer great difficulties in finding timely, essential care, with many doctors refusing to take Medicaid at all. Academic studies show the poor on Medicaid suffer worse health outcomes as a result, including premature death.[5] This is what seniors on Medicare will suffer when Medicare pays even less than Medicaid. As the Medicare actuaries put it in their understated, professional lingo, "the large reductions in Medicare payment rates to physicians would likely have serious implications for beneficiary access to care; utilization, intensity and quality of services; and other factors."[6]

On May 31, 2013, the Medicare actuaries released another report, estimating that by 2019 the Medicare cuts would result in "negative total facility margins for about 15 percent of hospitals, skilled nursing facilities, and home health agencies."[7] They further estimated that by 2030, 25 percent of hospitals and other health care providers would be suffering total losses as a result, and by 2050, 40 percent would.[8] The Medicare actuaries stated, "In practice, providers could not sustain continuing negative margins [total losses] and, absent legislative changes, would have to withdraw from providing services to Medicare beneficiaries" or somehow find others who would cover these huge losses, if possible.[9]

The annual reports for both the Medicare and Social Security programs include detailed year-by-year data from which we can calculate the exact future Medicare cuts under Obama's policies in current law. Comparing the reports from before Obamacare to the reports after Obamacare shows the Medicare cuts total $5 trillion over the next 20 years.[10]

Another official federal report, the *2010 Financial Report of the United States Government*, states regarding the impact of the Obamacare cuts on Medicare projections, "The 2010 projection is lower than the 2009 projection in every year of the projection period almost entirely as a result of the Affordable Care Act (ACA)."[11] Data presented later in that report repeatedly disclose the full present value of the future cuts in Medicare payments to doctors and hospitals for health care for seniors under Medicare: $15 trillion.[12]

Such draconian Medicare cuts would wreak havoc on in health care for seniors. Doctors, hospitals, surgeons, and specialists providing critical care to the elderly – surgery for hip and knee replacements, sophisticated diagnostics through MRIs and CT scans, and even treatment for cancer and heart disease – will either have to withdraw from serving Medicare patients or eventually go into bankruptcy. If the government is not going to pay sufficiently for health care under Medicare, seniors are not going to get the services, treatment, and care they have come to expect under Medicare. That is the natural outcome of these policies under Obamacare.

As Dr. Joseph Newhouse, a professor of health policy management at Harvard University, put it in an article for *Health Affairs*, these Medicare cuts "could jeopardize Medicare beneficiaries' access to mainstream medical care."[13] Timothy Jost, a professor of law at Washington and Lee University, wrote in the *New England Journal of Medicine*, "If the gap between private and Medicare rates continues to grow, health care providers may well abandon Medicare."[14] Even Peter Orszag, former director of the Office of Management and Budget (OMB) under Obama, wrote in *Foreign Affairs*, "If only Medicare and Medicaid payments were reduced, for example, providers would shift costs to other patients and also accept fewer Medicare and Medicaid patients."[15]

The Medicare actuaries believe these cuts will have such a severely negative impact on health care for seniors that Congress will be forced to reverse them, sharply increasing federal budget deficits. They write, "It is reasonable to expect that Congress will legislatively override or otherwise modify the reductions in the future to ensure that Medicare beneficiaries continue to have access to health care services."[16] They note the Medicare Board of Trustees, in its *2013 Medicare Trustees Report*,

> ... warns that "actual future Medicare expenditures are likely to exceed the intermediate projections shown in this report, possibly by quite large amounts." The Trustees Report is necessarily based on current law; as a result of questions regarding the operations of certain Medicare provisions [the Obamacare cuts], however, the projections shown in the report under current law are clearly unrealistic with respect to physician expenditures and, in addition,

may well understate expenditures for most other categories of
health care providers.[17]

The rest of the president's Medicare cuts are in payments to insurance
companies providing Medicare coverage and benefits to the nearly 30
percent of seniors who have chosen the option under Medicare Advantage,
otherwise known as Medicare Part C. Over the next 10 years the president's
health care law would cut payments to the insurance companies seniors
have chosen to provide this coverage by $156 billion.[18]

Cutter called these Medicare cuts "ending subsidies to insurance
companies." But would she call paying the manufacturers of the Air Force's
planes, the Navy's ships, and the Army's tanks "subsidies to arms
manufacturers?" They are simply payments for services rendered. The
Medicare Advantage cuts inevitably will lead to a loss of Medicare benefits
provided by these companies, just as reducing Medicare payments to
doctors and hospitals results in loss of health care services. That is why
those Medicare Advantage cuts were delayed until after the election.

But that is not all. Further cuts in Medicare may be adopted at will by
Obamacare's Independent Payment Advisory Board (IPAB). That board
will be composed of 15 unelected, appointed, Washington bureaucrats with
the power to adopt still more Medicare cuts that would go into effect
without the approval of Congress.[19] The IPAB bureaucrats have the
authority to cut Medicare payments to doctors and hospitals even more,
under a legal mandate requiring them to do so if necessary to keep Medicare
within certain arbitrary fiscal limits in future years.

Diane Cohen, former senior attorney at the Goldwater Institute, and
Michael F. Cannon, director of health policy studies at the Cato Institute,
say IPAB may be the most anti-constitutional measure ever to pass
Congress.[20] By anti-constitutional they mean worse than unconstitutional.
And that is a carefully restrained understatement compared to the
anti-democratic, authoritarian reality of IPAB.

The Obamacare law sets an annual target growth rate for Medicare
spending that is less than the annual growth of general health care inflation.
Whenever Medicare actuaries project the program will be growing faster
than the target rate, even if it is growing only at the rate of health care
inflation across the economy, Obamacare requires IPAB to issue a
"proposal" to cut Medicare some more, down to the target rate of growth.

Over the long term, in past years Medicare spending per senior has been growing 2.5 percent faster each year than the rate of growth of the economy.[21] IPAB is going to have a lot of cutting to do to bring that down to the legislated target rate each year.

To counter these burgeoning Medicare costs, IPAB has the power under Obamacare "to impose price controls [on health care] and other regulations, to impose taxes, and – despite disclaimers to the contrary – to ration care for all Americans, whether the government pays their medical bills or not," as Cohen and Cannon explain.[22] Although "IPAB's defenders note that PPACA explicitly prohibits IPAB's proposals from directly rationing health care," IPAB is fully empowered under Obamacare to "deny access to care as it sees fit simply by setting Medicare's prices for certain treatments and procedures so low that no providers will offer them," Cohen and Cannon further explain.[23] They add,

> This is hardly an abstraction. Under current law, by the end of the century Medicare's prices for hospital and physician services will fall from roughly 66 percent and 80 percent of what private insurers pay (respectively) to roughly one-third of what private insurers pay. These current-law price controls could result in "a serious decline in the availability and/or quality of health services for Medicare beneficiaries," according to Medicare's actuaries.[24]

IPAB's powers are not limited to such rationing under Medicare. IPAB is empowered to ration private health care across the entire economy. As Cohen and Cannon explain, Obamacare "requires IPAB to submit to Congress and the president recommendations to 'slow the growth in national health expenditures' and 'Non-Federal Health Care Programs.'" Cohen and Cannon add that Obamacare

> provides that if the Medicare actuaries project that the growth rate of national health expenditures will exceed that of per-enrollee Medicare spending, IPAB's "proposal shall be designed to help reduce the growth rate of [national health expenditures] while maintaining or enhancing beneficiary access to quality care under [Medicare]." This is a clear mandate to reduce both government and private-sector health care spending. Indeed, the simplest way to reduce overall health care spending while maintaining access to care for Medicare enrollees is to limit spending on patients outside

of Medicare.[25]

Moreover, if IPAB fails to act when required, including if the board is completely vacant without any members, Obamacare grants the secretary of the Department of Health and Human Services the authority to exercise all of IPAB's powers. That includes authority for the secretary to include additional funding for the secretary's office or HHS in IPAB "proposals," which again become automatically effective without the approval of Congress. Hence the Secretary can have the power to fund him- or herself or raise spending or even taxes simply on the order of the president to do so.

Obamacare purports to strictly limit the powers of Congress in response to any IPAB Medicare cuts or other action. Congress can reject any IPAB Medicare cuts, or other IPAB actions or proposals, only if it passes alternative measures that achieve the same savings. If Congress fails to do so within seven months, the IPAB actions or proposals automatically become law and the secretary of HHS is required to implement them. Cohen and Cannon explain, "When the unelected officials on this board [IPAB] submit a legislative proposal to Congress, it automatically becomes law."[26] They add,

> Blocking an IPAB "proposal" requires at a minimum that the House and the Senate and the president agree on a substitute. The Board's edicts therefore can become law without congressional action, congressional approval, meaningful congressional oversight, or being subject to a presidential veto. Citizens will have no power to challenge IPAB's edicts in court.[27]

Obamacare does not just strictly limit the power of Congress to respond to IPAB's actions or proposals. It purports to exempt IPAB from any judicial review whatsoever. As Cohen and Cannon summarize,

> The Act empowers IPAB's unelected government officials to propose legislation that can become law without congressional action, meaningful congressional oversight, and without being subject to a presidential veto, administrative review, or judicial review. The Act even attempts to prevent future Congresses from repealing IPAB.[28]

On this last point, Cohen and Cannon explain,

> Worse, PPACA forbids Congress from repealing IPAB outside of a seven-month window in the year 2017, and even then requires a three-fifths majority in both chambers. A heretofore unreported feature of PPACA dictates that if Congress misses that repeal window, PPACA prohibits Congress from ever altering an IPAB "proposal" [thereafter]. By restricting lawmaking powers of future Congresses, PPACA thus attempts to amend the Constitution by statute.[29]

Throwing out the separation of powers, Obamacare grants the president unprecedented power, taking us back before the Magna Carta, with monarchical power for the president to bypass Congress completely.

In other words, Obamacare's purported IPAB powers involve the closest thing to a *coup d'etat* in American history. It is more authoritarian and egregious than even the powers asserted by King George III, which inspired the first American Revolution. It takes America and Western Civilization all the way back to Julius Caesar.

Everyone who voted for Obamacare voted for these Medicare cuts and this *coup d'etat*. The point is not that there should never be cuts to future Medicare spending. The point is that Democrats cannot fairly criticize Republicans for dramatic future cuts to Medicare when the Democrats are already implementing precisely that today. Cutting trillions of dollars in Medicare payments to the doctors and hospitals actually providing health care to seniors, ultimately paying them less even than Medicaid, is not just a matter of cuts in "waste, fraud, and abuse," "overpayments," or "subsidies." It means seriously less health care for seniors when they are sick and most in need.

Most importantly, there is a much better way for seniors and taxpayers. Through structural reforms that introduce into Medicare market incentives and competition, and real savings and investment, seniors can get more and better health care than they can with today's Medicare. At the same time, taxpayers would save much more than they would with the Obamacare Medicare cuts, which are actually going to finance much more spending under Obamacare.

The Overwhelming Financial Crisis of Medicare

The Hospital Insurance (HI) portion of Medicare, known as Medicare Part A, "helps pay for hospital, home health following hospital stays, skilled nursing facility, and hospice care for the aged and disabled."[30] It is the part of Medicare financed by the Medicare payroll tax, which is 2.9 percent of wage income without limit. Obamacare imposes an additional surcharge, increasing that payroll tax to 3.8 percent for singles earning more than $200,000 per year and couples earning $250,000 or more per year.

Those income thresholds are not indexed to increase over time, so eventually the higher tax rate, representing a 31 percent increase in Medicare payroll taxes, will apply to 80 percent of all workers, according to the Medicare actuaries.[31] That constitutes a substantial tax increase on future middle-income households, breaking a campaign promise made by Obama and congressional Democrats. In addition, Obamacare applies this 3.8 percent payroll tax to investment income for the first time. Investment income is taxed by the individual income tax, the corporate income tax, the capital gains tax, the dividends tax, the death tax, and now the Medicare payroll tax.

This is why African-American unemployment has remained in double digits for every year Obama has been president, Hispanic unemployment remained close to double digits going into Obama's sixth year as president, poverty has soared during his administration, the take-home pay of middle-income households has declined every year of the Obama presidency, there has been no real economic recovery from the recession back to normal U.S. economic growth under Obama, and under current economic policies the nation's children have no real economic future.

Despite those tax increases and the draconian, intractable, unworkable cuts in Medicare payments to doctors and hospitals, HI continued to run a deficit in 2013, as it has since 2008 and is projected to continue to do in 2014.[32] By 2022, under intermediate assumptions, the cash flow deficit for Medicare Part A alone, counting the interest on the HI trust fund bonds, which is also paid by federal taxpayers, is projected to be $40.7 billion.[33]

Medicare's actuaries project that under so-called "intermediate" assumptions, continued deficits will completely exhaust the HI trust fund by 2026, just 11 years from now, when, absent other reforms, Medicare Part A benefits under current law would have to be immediately reduced to the level of current HI payroll tax income.[34] "Beneficiary access to health care services would rapidly be curtailed," the *Medicare Trustees Report* states.[35] Under so-called "pessimistic" assumptions, this exhaustion of the HI trust fund would occur in 2019, just four years from now.[36]

Continuing to pay all promised Medicare Part A benefits would require ultimately doubling Medicare payroll tax rates from their current level, under what the government's actuaries call intermediate assumptions.[37] Under pessimistic assumptions, current HI payroll tax rates would have to be increased roughly fourfold, to around 13 percent, just for Medicare Part A alone.[38]

The Supplementary Medical Insurance (SMI) portion of Medicare, known as Medicare Part B, "helps pay for physician, outpatient hospital, home health, and other services for the aged and disabled. ..." Part B is financed primarily by premiums paid by seniors, covering about 24 percent of Part B expenses today, and general revenues, currently explicitly covering about 68 percent of Part B expenses (general revenues are actually covering 76 percent of Part B expenses today).[39] By 2022, under intermediate assumptions, the general revenue contributions for Medicare Part B, plus the interest on the SMI trust fund bonds, are projected to total $383.5 billion.[40]

The Medicare actuaries project Part B, on its current course without reform, will ultimately consume approximately 25 percent of all federal personal and corporate income taxes.[41] Adding in the Part A deficits means Medicare deficits alone, on the program's current course without reform, would eventually total close to one-third of all federal personal and corporate income taxes.

Medicare Part D is the prescription drug insurance program, in which about 10 percent of program costs are financed by premiums paid by seniors; the rest is covered by general revenue contributions. By 2022, under intermediate assumptions, general revenue contributions for Part D are projected to total $123.2 billion.[42]

Consequently, Medicare's total deficits, requiring general revenue financing, are projected under intermediate assumptions to reach $547.4 billion by 2022, in that one year alone, just for this one federal program.

The Medicare actuaries confess this calculation is likely to be a serious underestimate of the long-term financing crisis. Even the actuaries admit the Obamacare Medicare cuts, on top of other automatic Medicare spending restraint provisions, "may be difficult to sustain" because they would be so draconian in their effect on seniors' health care.[43]

For more than 10 years, Congress has routinely delayed the effects of the sustainable growth rate (SGR) formula for restraining the growth of physician fee schedules under Medicare, fearing the effects those fee cuts would have on the quality and availability of health care for seniors. If they went into effect today, the cumulative delayed effects of the SGR fee cuts would represent a fee cut of 25 percent for doctors providing health care for seniors under Medicare. The Medicare financial projections noted above all assume that sharp fee cut took place in 2014.

The Medicare actuaries do not believe Congress will ever allow the SGR fee cut to go into effect. The *2013 Medicare Trustees Report* states, "it is a virtual certainty that lawmakers, cognizant of the disruptive consequences of such a sudden, sharp reduction in payments, will override this reduction as they have every year since 2003."[44]

On top of that, Obamacare calls for additional "reductions in the annual payment rate updates for most categories of Medicare providers [doctors and hospitals] by the growth in economy-wide multifactor productivity."[45] The *2013 Medicare Trustees Report* states,

> [I]f the health sector cannot transition to more efficient models of care delivery and achieve productivity increases commensurate with economy-wide productivity, and if the provider reimbursement rates paid by commercial insurers continue to follow the same negotiated process used to date, then the availability and quality of health care received by Medicare beneficiaries would, under current law, fall over time relative to that received by those with private health insurance."[46]

Precisely because the Obamacare Medicare fee cuts are likely to have dramatic negative effects on health care for seniors, the actuaries think Congress is likely to sharply curtail those cuts, just as Congress has delayed implementation of the SGR fee cuts for so many years.

The Medicare actuaries, in fact, have developed and published an "alternative scenario" reflecting what they think will really happen with the Obamacare Medicare cuts. In that alternative scenario, spending for Medicare Part A (HI) ultimately soars by 142 percent, much more than double, as a percent of taxable payroll. HI payroll taxes also much more than double, rising by 142 percent as well, to close to 10 percent of personal income.[47] Medicare Part B (SMI) would ultimately rise by 165 percent as a percent of GDP, again much more than doubling.[48] Total Medicare spending would grow by 156 percent as a percent of GDP, also much more than doubling.[49]

The pre-Obamacare *2009 Medicare Trustees Report* shows fully what Medicare's finances would look like without the Obamacare Medicare cuts. The unfunded liability for Medicare Part A alone was estimated at $36.4 trillion.[50] The present value of future general revenue requirements for Medicare Part B, which is another measure of unfunded liabilities, was estimated at $37 trillion.[51] The present value of future general revenue requirements for Medicare Part D was estimated at $15.5 trillion.

So the total present unfunded liabilities of Medicare today, without the Obamacare cuts the Medicare actuaries say Congress is unlikely to make because they would deny seniors access to health care, may be calculated as $89 trillion.

Ryan's Medicare vs. Obamacare's Medicare

The Medicare reform plan proposed by Rep. Paul Ryan (R-WI) would deal with this long-term Medicare financing crisis in a far better way for seniors and taxpayers. It would allow workers under age 55 today to choose when they retire a private plan competing alongside traditional Medicare. Medicare would provide these seniors with a premium support payment they could use to pay for or offset the premium of the private plan they choose. That premium support payment would be set by competitive bidding under rules ensuring it will be enough to pay for at least two of the competing plans providing at least the same benefits as Medicare.

Seniors would have market incentives to choose the lowest-cost plans, but they would be free to choose higher-cost plans with more and better benefits than Medicare, supplementing the premium support payment they get from Medicare with their own funds. Market competition and incentives would drive the private plans to innovate to keep costs down, and each senior would always remain free to choose the current Medicare system instead of any of the competing private plans.

Seniors also would be free to choose highly popular health savings accounts (HSAs) for their Medicare coverage, maximizing the control they have over their own health care. HSAs have proven highly effective in controlling costs in the real world, through the market incentives they include for patients, doctors, and hospitals.

Under Ryan's reform plan, moreover, additional supplements to the

Medicare premium support would be provided for lower-income and less-healthy seniors. This would help create market competition among private insurers to best serve the seniors in most need, who would enter the market with additional funds to pay for their additional needed care.

During the 2012 presidential campaign, Obama was quoted as saying, "[the Ryan] voucher plan for Medicare would bankrupt Medicare. Our plan strengthens Medicare." CBO, however, scores the Ryan plan as reducing the growth of Medicare spending from currently projected levels by 0.75 percent of GDP by 2030, 1.5 percent of GDP by 2040, and 2.5 percent of GDP by 2050, unambiguously strengthening Medicare.[52] Those savings are achieved by the operation of incentives, competition, and senior choice, as opposed to the payment cuts imposed under Obamacare. There are no grounds for saying the reforms would bankrupt Medicare.

By "our plan," Obama meant Obamacare – which raids Medicare for at least $716 billion, primarily in cuts to payments to doctors and hospitals, as discussed above. That raid does not in any way strengthen Medicare but rather greatly weakens the ability of Medicare to deliver the health care seniors have come to expect.

David Cutler, a former advisor to Presidents Obama and Bill Clinton, alleges health care costs for current and future seniors would increase dramatically under the Ryan Medicare reforms. But that allegation is not accurate, because under the Ryan plan the premium support for seniors each year would be set by competitive bidding at the second-lowest bid from the competing private plans. That means the premium support would always be enough for each senior to choose at least two plans offering the same benefits as Medicare at no extra cost to them. Seniors would bear a higher cost only if they chose a more expensive plan providing benefits they think are worth the extra cost.

All Ryan's Medicare reforms would do, in fact, is extend to the old-fashioned Medicare Parts A and B the popular and successful policies of the more modern Medicare Parts C and D.

Medicare Part D is the prescription drug program. Just like Ryan's proposed Medicare reforms, Part D provides premium support payments to seniors, which they use to purchase the private prescription drug coverage of their choice. Because of the private market competition and incentives for seniors to choose lower-cost plans, Part D costs have run 40 percent below projections. Compare that to Parts A and B, which by 1990 cost 10 times the original projections for that year when the program was adopted.

Medicare Part C is Medicare Advantage, under which nearly 30 percent of seniors already have chosen private insurance to provide all their Medicare coverage. Seniors believe they get a better deal through this highly popular program due to choice and competition.

As the Reuters news service has documented, the origins of Ryan's Medicare reform plan are found in work by Washington liberals Robert Reischauer, former director of CBO, and Henry Aaron of the Brookings Institution.[53] They were the first to propose a premium support system for Medicare, in a 1995 article in the journal *Health Affairs*.[54] Ryan's Medicare reforms have drawn support from Alice Rivlin, the liberal godmother of CBO and its first director, and from liberal Democrat Sen. Ron Wyden of Oregon, who sponsored a Senate version of Ryan's plan.

During the 2012 campaign, Obama also was quoted as saying Ryan and GOP presidential candidate Mitt Romney wanted to "give money back to insurance companies and put them in charge of Medicare." Ryan's Medicare reforms, however, would not put insurance companies in charge of Medicare any more than Medicare Parts C and D involve putting insurance companies in charge of Medicare.

The Centers for Medicare and Medicaid Services remain in charge, requiring each competing insurance plan to provide at least the same benefits as Medicare does today. In addition, each senior is in charge of making his or her own choice of where to get Medicare benefits, as is true under Medicare Parts C and D today. If a senior chooses a private competing plan, the government pays that plan to provide the benefits, as determined by competitive bidding, as is true under Medicare Parts C and D today. That is not "giving money back to insurance companies" any more than any other government procurement action involves "giving money back" to the companies that provide the desired good or service.

Ryan's reforms would reduce the projected explosive growth in Medicare spending through market competition, incentives, and senior choice, resulting in a much better Medicare for seniors.

Obamacare would raid Medicare through arbitrary, draconian cuts in payments to the doctors and hospitals that provide health care to seniors. Ryan's reforms would allow seniors to escape these draconian cuts. They would choose from among competing private health plans that must pay doctors and hospitals adequately to attract customers for their health insurance: If their customers can't get health care with their insurance, those health plans are not going to have many customers.

Personal Accounts for Medicare

An additional reform should be added to Ryan's plan to fully reinforce the system's fiscal foundation and provide even better benefits for retirees: Workers should be free to put the Medicare payroll taxes they and their employers currently pay into their own personal savings, investment, and insurance accounts, under the same framework as proposed in Chapter 2 for Social Security.

Just as with personal accounts for Social Security, workers would choose investments by picking a fund managed by a private investment firm, from a list officially approved for this purpose and regulated for safety and soundness. That would follow the personal account savings and investment system used in Chile, which pioneered private market savings, investment, and insurance as an alternative for social insurance more than 30 years ago.

Companies that wanted to offer investment funds would apply to the U.S. Treasury Department for approval of the company itself and the particular investment funds it wanted to offer. The investment funds would be required to be highly diversified for investment safety, but they could be invested in a broad range of stocks and bonds and other investments to maximize returns and benefits for workers. The personal account investments would be kept strictly separate from the rest of the company, as is done in Chile, so any financial troubles the company might experience would have no effect on the personal account investments.

When the worker retires, the accumulated Medicare personal account funds would finance an annuity payment to supplement the Ryan Medicare premium support payments in paying for the private health plan the retiree chooses. Because Medicare payroll taxes today finance about one-third of total Medicare spending, a worker who exercised the Medicare personal account option for his or her entire career would forego about one-third of the Medicare premium support payment in retirement, with the funds from the annuity paying substantially more than that even if they earned only standard long-term market returns over the worker's career. For workers who exercise the personal account option for a smaller proportion of their careers, the Medicare premium support payments would be proportionately larger. The continuing Medicare premium support payments would be financed primarily by the remaining Medicare revenues that finance roughly two-thirds of Medicare spending today, and general revenues, just like in the transition to Social Security personal accounts discussed in Chapter 2.[55]

An early, detailed proposal for personal accounts for Medicare was developed by John C. Goodman, at the time president of the National Center for Policy Analysis, in 2008.[56] That model included a health savings account (HSA) option for Medicare, bringing all the benefits of the powerful cost-saving incentives of such HSAs. It gave doctors and hospitals more pricing freedom for their health services to respond to consumers with HSA cost-saving incentives. And it provided for a Medicare personal account for 4 percent of taxable payroll.

Goodman concluded his proposal would eliminate the long-term deficits of Medicare. Medicare spending would be reduced sharply by the HSA incentives and because the personal accounts would finance so much of it through private savings, investment, and insurance rather than through taxes. And this calculation does not include the substantial long-term spending savings from the Ryan premium-support reforms.

Clearly, the otherwise-intractable long-term Medicare financing crisis can be solved without tax increases or Medicare benefit cuts, instead using market competition, incentives, senior choice, and the consequences of personal account savings, investment, and insurance. The 2008 NCPA study concluded that under the reforms it proposed, the proportion of Medicare spending funded through taxes would ultimately decline from 86 percent today to 25 percent after 75 years. The rest would be financed through private savings, investment, and insurance, eliminating most of the unfunded liabilities of Medicare entirely through this means alone.

On our current course without reform, Medicare spending would ultimately consume close to three times as much of our national income as it does today. Under the NCPA reforms the share of national income taken by Medicare would not rise at all. The enormous long-term Medicare financing gaps of today can be eliminated entirely without tax increases, or cutting Medicare benefits, or any increased economic burden on seniors.

Conclusion

Even Medicare, which presents the most difficult entitlement reform problem of all, can be fixed in a way that benefits seniors and taxpayers alike, through fundamental structural reforms. Instead of raising taxes or cutting Medicare benefits, the current enormous, intractable, long-term Medicare deficits can be eliminated entirely through market incentives, competition, senior choice, and personal account savings, investment, and insurance. Together, those structural reform measures would reduce

Medicare spending over the long run by more than 50 percent from where it would be otherwise.

Seniors would enjoy a better Medicare than they have today. Instead of suffering dramatic reductions in Medicare payments to the doctors and hospitals that provide their health care, seniors would be free to have the private health insurance of their own choice, with sufficient payments to medical providers to ensure there would be no reduction in the quality of their health care.

These Medicare reforms also would contribute powerfully to increased economic growth and prosperity. Instead of sharp tax rate increases that reduce economic growth, the burden of health costs would be sharply reduced through market competition and incentives. In addition, the personal account savings, investment, and insurance would contribute substantial savings and capital investment to the economy, promoting economic growth and prosperity for all.

Notes

1. Letter to the Honorable Nancy Pelosi from Douglas Elmendorf, director, Congressional Budget Office, March 20, 2010; Richard S. Foster, chief actuary, Estimated Financial Effects of the "Patient Protection and Affordable Care Act," as Amended, Centers for Medicare and Medicaid Services, U.S. Department of Health and Human Services, April 22, 2010.

2. Transcript of the First Presidential Debate, *The New York Times*, October 3, 2012.

3. Peter Ferrara, *What Cuts Will Be Made to Medicare and How It Will Affect Seniors, Part 2, Reality Check*, A Project of the National Center for Policy Analysis, August 29, 2012.

4. John D. Shatto and Kent Clemens, *Projected Medicare Expenditures under an Illustrative Scenario with Alternative Payment Updates to Medicare Providers*, Office of the Actuary, Centers for Medicare and Medicaid Services, August 5, 2010, p. 5.

5. Scott Gottlieb, "Medicaid Is Worse Than No Coverage at All," *The Wall Street Journal*, March 10, 2011; Siran M. Koroukian, Ph.D., Paul M. Bakaki, M.D., M.S., and Derek Raghavan, M.D., Ph.D., "Survival Disparities by Medicaid Status: An Analysis of 8 Cancers," *Cancer* 118, no. 17 (September 1, 2012): 4271–9; Damien J. LaPar, M.D., *et al.*, "Primary Payer Status Affects Mortality for Major Surgical Operations," *Annals of Surgery* 252, no. 3 (September 2010): 544–51; Jeremiah G. Allen, *et al.*, "Insurance and education predict long-term survival after orthotopic heart transplantation in the United States," *The Journal of Heart and Lung Transplantation* 31, no. 1 (January 2012): 52–60; Sally C. Pipes, *The Truth About Obamacare* (Washington, DC: Regnery, 2010), pp. 76, 86.

6. Shatto and Clemens, *supra* note 4, p. 12.

7. John D. Shatto and Kent Clemens, *Projected Medicare Expenditures under Illustrative Scenarios with Alternative Payment Updates to Medicare Providers*, Office of the Actuary, Centers for Medicare and Medicaid Services, May 31, 2013, pp. 8–9.

8. *Ibid.*, p. 9.

9. *Ibid.*

10. *2009 Annual Report of the Boards of Trustees of the Federal Hospital Insurance and Federal Supplementary Medical Insurance Trust Funds*, May 12, 2009; 2010 *Annual Report of the Boards of Trustees of the Federal Hospital Insurance and Federal Supplementary Medical Insurance Trust Funds*, August 5, 2010.

11. U.S. Department of the Treasury, *2010 Financial Report of the United States Government*, December 2010, pp. ix, 19.

12. *Ibid.* In Table 1 on p. 3, the present value of net expenditures for Medicare is shown as declining from $38.1 trillion in 2009 to $22.8 trillion in 2010, a decline of $15.3 trillion. In Table 8 on pp. 20–21, the net social insurance expenditures are projected to decline from $46 trillion in the 2009 report to $31 trillion in the 2010 report. On pp. 46–48, United States Government Statements of Social Insurance show the present value of future expenditures for Medicare Part A declining from $25.8 trillion in

2009 to $17.1 trillion in 2010; present value of future expenditures for Medicare Part B declines from $23.2 trillion in 2009 to $17.7 trillion in 2010; and total present values of future expenditures in excess of future revenues for social insurance declines from $45.9 trillion to 30.9 trillion.

13. Joseph P. Newhouse, "Assessing Health Reform's Impact on Four Key Groups of Americans," *Health Affairs* 29, no. 9 (July 22, 2010): 1–11.

14. Timothy Jost, "The Independent Payment Advisory Board," *New England Journal of Medicine* 362, no. 2 (July 8, 2010): 103–5.

15. Peter R. Orzag, "How Health Care Can Save or Sink America," *Foreign Affairs* 90, no. 4 (July/August 2011): 42–56.

16. Shatto and Clemens, *supra* note 4, pp. 1–2.

17. *Ibid.*, p. 1.

18. Letter to the Honorable Nancy Pelosi from Douglas Elmendorf, *supra* note 1.

19. Diane Cohen and Michael F. Cannon, "The Independent Payment Advisory Board, PPACA's Anti-Constitutional and Authoritarian Super-Legislature," *Cato Policy Analysis* No. 700, Cato Institute, June 14, 2012.

20. *Ibid.*, p. 1.

21. U.S. Congressional Budget Office, *The Long-Term Budget Outlook*, August 2010, p. 33.

22. Cohen and Cannon, *supra* note 19, p. 5.

23. *Ibid.*

24. *Ibid.*

25. *Ibid.*, p. 7.

26. *Ibid.*, p. 1.

27. *Ibid.*

28. *Ibid.*, p. 3.

29. *Ibid.*

30. *2013 Annual Report of the Boards of Trustees of the Federal Hospital Insurance and Federal Supplementary Medical Insurance Trust Funds*, May 21, 2013, p. 1.

31. *Ibid.*, p. 30.

32. *Ibid.*, p. 6.

33. *Ibid.*, p. 58.

34. *Ibid.*, p. 6.

35. *Ibid.*, p. 28.

36. *Ibid.*, p. 29.

37. *Ibid.*, Table VI.F.2., p. 195.

38. *Ibid.*, Table VI.F.2, p. 196.

39. *Ibid.*, Table II.B1, p. 10.

40. *Ibid.*, p. 90.

41. *Ibid.*, Table II.F3, p. 43.

42. *Ibid.*, p. 111.

43. *Ibid.*, p. 2.

44. *Ibid.*

45. *Ibid.*, p. 3.

46. *Ibid.*

47. Shatto and Clemens, *supra* note 4, p. 14.

48. *Ibid.*, Table 4, p. 18.

49. *Ibid.*, Table 5. p. 19.

50. *2009 Medicare Trustees Report*, *supra* note 10, Table III.B10.

51. *Ibid.*, Table III.C15.

52. Congressional Budget Office, *A Premium Support System for Medicare, Analysis of Illustrative Options*, September 18, 2013.

53. David Morgan, "Republican Plan for Medicare Could Face Years of Hurdles – Experts," Reuters News Service, September 10, 2012.

54. H.J. Aaron and R.D. Reischauer, "The Medicare reform debate: what is the next step?" *Health Affairs* 14, no. 4 (1995): 8–30.

55. The Medicare personal accounts would involve a transition-financing cash-flow burden, as would the Social Security personal accounts. That transition would be financed by the savings generated by the rest of the entitlement reforms described in this book, as would be the case with the Social Security personal accounts.

56. John C. Goodman, "A Framework for Medicare Reform," *NCPA Policy Report* No. 315, National Center for Policy Analysis, September 2008.

4

Block Grants for All: Liberating the Poor and Taxpayers Alike

America's welfare state is not just a principality; it is a vast empire bigger than the entire budget of almost every other country in the world. That empire involves nearly 200 joint federal and state means-tested welfare programs, including Medicaid, food stamps, 27 low-income housing programs, 30 employment and training programs, 34 social services programs, another dozen food and nutrition programs, another 22 low-income health programs, and 24 low-income child care programs, among others.

Just one program, Medicaid, cost federal and state taxpayers $453 billion in 2013, a figure projected to soar to $664 billion per year by 2018. Under the Patient Protection and Affordable Care Act, also known as Obamacare, 85 million Americans will soon be on Medicaid, growing to nearly 100 million by 2021.[1] And there are at least 184 additional, widely recognized, means-tested federal welfare programs, most jointly financed and administered with the states.

In addition to Medicaid is the State Children's Health Insurance Program (SCHIP). Another such program is food stamps, now officially called the Supplemental Nutrition Assistance Program (SNAP). Nearly 50 million Americans were receiving food stamps in 2013. That is nearly one in seven Americans, up 50 percent just since President Barack Obama entered office in January 2009.[2] Federal spending on food stamps totaled $78 billion in 2011, double the $36 billion spent just three years earlier in 2008.

SNAP is not the only federal nutrition program for the needy. There is the Special Supplemental Nutrition Program for Women, Infants, and Children (WIC), which targets assistance to pregnant women and mothers with small children. There are the means-tested School Breakfast Program and School Lunch Program. There is the Summer Food Service Program for Children. There are the lower-income components of the Child and Adult Care Food Program, the Emergency Food Assistance Program, and the Commodity Supplemental Food Program (CSFP). Then there is the Nutrition Program for the Elderly. All told, the nation's taxpayers provide literally cradle-to-grave food service for tens of millions of people. In 2013, federal spending for food and nutrition assistance overall reached more than $100 billion for the first time, to $104.5 billion.

Then there is federal housing assistance, totaling $57.6 billion in 2013. This includes expenditures for more than one million public housing units owned by the government. It includes Section 8 rental assistance for nearly another four million private housing units. There are Rural Rental Assistance, Rural Housing Loans, and Rural Rental Housing Loans. Also included are Home Investment Partnerships (HOME), Community Development Block Grants (CDBG), Housing for Special Populations (Elderly and Disabled), Housing Opportunities for Persons with AIDS (HOPWA), Emergency Shelter Grants, the Supportive Housing program, the Single Room Occupancy program, the Shelter Plus Care program, and the Home Ownership and Opportunity for People Everywhere (HOPE) program, among others.

In addition to medical care, food, and housing, the federal government also provides cash. The old New Deal-era Aid to Families with Dependent Children (AFDC) is now Temporary Assistance for Needy Families (TANF), which pays cash mostly to single mothers with children. There is also the Earned Income Tax Credit (EITC), which sends low-income workers checks even though they usually owe no taxes to be credited against. The Child Tax Credit similarly provides cash to families with children. The Supplemental Security Income (SSI) program provides cash for the low-income aged, blind, and disabled. In 2013 such income security programs accounted for nearly another $155 billion in federal spending.

The federal government also provides means-tested assistance through multiple programs for child care, education, job training, and the Low Income Home Energy Assistance Program (LIHEAP), the Social Services Block Grant, the Community Services Block Grant, and the Legal Services Corporation, among other programs.

Federal and state governments spend a trillion dollars a year on these means-tested welfare programs, not including Social Security and Medicare.[3] That is roughly $17,000 per person in poverty, more than $50,000 for a family of three. The Census Bureau estimates our current welfare spending totals four times what would be necessary just to give all of the poor enough cash to bring them up to the poverty line.[4] Charles Murray of the American Enterprise Institute wrote an entire book, *In Our Hands*, documenting that we spend through government programs far more than enough to completely eliminate all poverty in the United States.[5] This dramatic overspending leaves wide scope for reforms that would be far more effective in reducing poverty while saving taxpayers a fortune.

Over the 10-year period from 2009 to 2018, federal and state welfare spending will total $10.3 trillion.[6] This does not include Obamacare's expansion of Medicaid, the new Obamacare entitlement that provides health insurance subsidies for families making close to $100,000 per year, and other such expensive provisions. Together, this abusive entitlement spending will add trillions more to the federal budget.

Even in 2005, government spending on these means-tested welfare programs was 25 percent more than was spent on national defense, and that was at the height of the wars in the Middle East.[7] Government overall – federal, state, and local – spends more only on the big entitlements for retirees – Social Security and Medicare – and on primary, secondary, and postsecondary education.[8] Indeed, total welfare spending may have outpaced spending on education by now.

Over the past two decades, total welfare spending has been growing faster than spending on Social Security and Medicare, about twice as fast as spending on education, and nearly three times as fast as spending on national defense.[9] By 2013, total government spending on welfare was 50 percent more than spending for national defense under Obama's budget policies.

The War on Poverty famously began in 1965. From 1965 to 2008, nearly $16 trillion was spent on means-tested welfare for the poor (in 2008 dollars).[10] The Heritage Foundation's Robert Rector and his colleagues report that was much more than all spending on all military conflicts from the American Revolution to today, which total $6.39 trillion in 2008 dollars.[11] The total cost of World War II in 2008 dollars was $4.1 trillion, about one-fourth as much as was spent on the War on Poverty.[12] Since the War on Poverty began, total annual inflation-adjusted welfare spending has soared by 13 times, or 1,200 percent, while the total U.S. population has grown by only 50 percent.[13]

What have we gotten in return for all that spending? Poverty fell sharply before the War on Poverty, after the Great Depression and World War II. The poverty rate fell from 32 percent in 1950 to 22.4 percent in 1959 to 12.1 percent in 1969, soon after the War on Poverty programs went into effect. Progress against poverty, as measured by the poverty rate, then abruptly stopped.

The poverty rate bounced up and down around that 1969 level throughout the 1970s, before starting to rise again in the late '70s. From 1978 to 1982, the poverty rate rose by almost a third, to 15.0 percent, reflecting the chaotic economy of the 1970s. It fell below the 1969 level only once, briefly, during the three-year period 1999 to 2001. In 2012, the U.S. poverty rate was back up to 15 percent, about where it was when the War on Poverty began, despite the expenditure of $16 trillion. In other words, we fought the War on Poverty, and poverty won.

But it's not all gloom and doom. Something has been working for the poor. In addition to reporting the official poverty rate, the Census Bureau collects comprehensive data on the living conditions of the poor. Rector regularly reviews those data and issues reports on the material condition of the poor in modern America. As Rector explained in his 2007 report,[14] the Census Bureau data show 43 percent of all poor households own their own home. The average home owned by the poor is a three-bedroom house with one-and-a-half baths, a garage, and a porch or patio. The typical poor American has more living space than the average non-poor individual living in Athens, London, Paris, Vienna, and other cities throughout Europe. About half of America's poor live in single-family homes. Only 6 percent of poor households are overcrowded, with more than one person per room; two-thirds have more than two rooms per person.

The average consumption of protein, vitamins, and minerals is virtually the same for the children of poor and middle-income families, Rector continues, and in most cases is well above recommended norms. Poor children consume more meat than do higher-income children and enjoy average protein intakes 100 percent above recommended levels. Overconsumption of calories is the biggest nutrition problem among the poor, as it is with the general U.S. population. Most poor children today are, in fact, "super-nourished," as Rector puts it. Today's poor children consequently grow up to be, on average, one inch taller and 10 pounds heavier than the GIs who stormed the beaches of Normandy in World War II, as Rector further observes. As to hunger, 89 percent of the poor report their families have enough food to eat, while only 1.5 percent say they often do not have enough to eat.

Nearly three-quarters of poor households in the United States own a car, and nearly a third own two or more cars. In addition, 80 percent of poor U.S. households have air conditioning, whereas in 1970 only 36 percent of the entire U.S. population enjoyed air conditioning. Moreover, 97 percent of poor households own a color TV, with more than half owning two or more; 78 percent own a VCR or DVD player; 62 percent have cable or satellite TV; 89 percent own microwave ovens; more than half own a stereo; and more than a third own personal computers and automatic dishwashers. A third of poor households have both cellular and landline phones.

Rector notes the typical poor family with children is supported by only 800 hours of work per year, which amounts to 16 hours per week. If work in each family were raised to 2,000 hours per year, the equivalent of one adult working 40 hours per week throughout the year, nearly 75 percent of the nation's poor children would be lifted out of poverty.[15]

The Poverty of Welfare

Even though the poor in America don't live in material suffering, they nevertheless do suffer a real poverty. Not a poverty of material conditions, though there is some real material deprivation among some of the poor, but a poverty of social conditions, which does involve real misery. The root cause of that poverty is the perverse, counterproductive incentives arising from the welfare system itself.

In 1984, Charles Murray's book *Losing Ground* shocked the nation by documenting how thoroughly we did indeed lose the War on Poverty. He showed that on a wide range of key social indicators – such as work, marriage, out-of-wedlock births, crime, and alcohol and drug abuse, among others – the condition of the bulk of the poor actually worsened in response to the massive increase in government welfare programs that started in the mid-1960s with the War on Poverty.

One key reason poverty stopped declining after the War on Poverty was launched is that the poor and lower-income population stopped working, leading to the deteriorating social conditions Murray cites. In 1960, nearly two-thirds of U.S. households in the lowest-income one-fifth of the population were headed by persons who worked.[16] By 1991, this work effort had declined by about 50 percent, with only one-third of household heads in the bottom 20 percent in income working and only 11 percent working full-time, year-round.[17]

This was not a matter of the poor not being able to find work. Although the economy was chaotic during the 1970s, during the 1980s and 1990s the United States enjoyed a historic economic boom creating millions of jobs. The proof is in how people voted with their feet. Millions of illegal immigrants surged across the U.S. border to gain those jobs and participate in America's economic golden age, with the unemployment rate collapsing into insignificance by the end of the 1990s and into the early 2000s.

With the government offering generous and wide-ranging welfare benefits, from housing to medical care to food stamps to outright cash, naturally many choose to reduce or eliminate their work effort and take the benefits. In terms of incentives, it is as if the government is paying people not to work and rewarding them for having low incomes. To distinguish this from other perverse incentives of welfare, I call this the "whirlpool effect," as it sucks the poor and low-income individuals down deeper into long-term poverty and an intergenerational increase of social pathologies.

A seminal study by the federal government in the 1970s confirms this argument. Under the experiment, the government provided special, even-more-generous packages of welfare benefits to groups of beneficiaries in Seattle and Denver. The welfare packages included everything liberal policymakers could hope for, effectively providing a generous guaranteed income. Conducted from 1971 to 1978, the effort became known as the Seattle/Denver Income Maintenance Experiment, or "SIME/DIME."

The dramatic bottom-line result: For every $1 of extra welfare given to low-income persons, they reduced their labor and earnings by 80 cents.[18] No wonder the War on Poverty failed.

The Poverty Trap

Welfare benefits from the various programs typically phase out at between 150 percent and 200 percent of the poverty level, affecting about one-third of the workforce. This creates another work-disincentive problem, labeled by economists Arthur Laffer and Stephen Moore as the "poverty trap."[19] As welfare is phased out as income rises, the loss of welfare benefits is economically the same as a tax on the rising earnings.

Consider the example of someone in poverty who receives $12,000 a year in welfare benefits. Suppose she gets the opportunity for a job earning

$16,000 a year. If she loses 50 cents in welfare benefits for every dollar earned, that is like a 50 percent tax taking away $8,000 of her earnings from work. The payroll tax will take another 7.65 percent of her earnings, federal income taxes another 10 percent on the margin, and state income taxes roughly another 5 percent on the margin on average. That leaves an effective marginal tax rate of 72.65 percent, leaving little incentive for the poor to work.

Laffer and Moore write,

> Needs tests, means tests, and income tests exclude people [from welfare] as their incomes progressively increase, ensuring that funds are not squandered on those who are less in need. While "needs" tests may be rationalized on both moral and budgetary grounds, when combined with payroll and income taxes, the phased reduction of welfare benefits has meant that spendable income actually rises very little as gross wages increase, and for some income thresholds, spendable income (total spending power) actually declines as wages increase.[20]

The true reality of the poverty trap is actually worse than in the example just discussed above. In a trailblazing paper in 1983, Laffer examined the total effect of all the needs tests and taxes affecting an inner-city family of four on welfare in Los Angeles.[21] He found,

> What was clear from this analysis is that marginal tax rates for inner city inhabitants were prohibitively high – in some cases, the poorest people actually faced the highest marginal tax rates of all income groups. Over the entire range from no wages to wages of $1,300 per month, the family in my analysis faced marginal tax rates ... that ranged from a low of 53 percent (a poor family gained only $47 in spendable income when its gross monthly wages increased from $0 to $100) to a high of 314 percent (a poor family lost $214 in spendable income when its gross monthly wages increased from $1,000 to $1,100 a month.[22]

A 1996 Urban Institute study by Linda Ginnarelli and Eugene Steuerle similarly found the poor faced effective marginal tax rates of 70 percent to 101 percent.[23] The authors state, "A significant portion of the population faces tax rates of 100 percent or more for work at a full-time minimum wage job or for increasing their work effort beyond some minimal level. The net impact of this system, in our view, is pernicious."[24]

Laffer and Moore cite a blog item by economics professor Jeff Frankel of Harvard University's Kennedy School of Government, who recounts this anecdote of a single mother:

> She had moved from a $25,000 a year job to a $35,000 a year job, and suddenly she couldn't make ends meet any more. ... She really did come out behind by several hundred dollars a month. She lost free health insurance and instead had to pay $230 a month for her employer-provided health insurance. Her rent associated with her section 8 voucher went up by 30% of the income gain (which is the rule). She lost the ($280 a month) subsidized child care voucher she had for after school child care for her child. She lost around $1600 a year of the EITC. She paid payroll tax on the additional income. Finally, the new job was in Boston, and she lived in a suburb. So now she has $300 a month of additional gas and parking charges.[25]

The National Center for Children in Poverty similarly reported the financial incentives faced by a single mother with two children living in Philadelphia:

> Even with the help of government work supports, Becky can't cover her family's basic expenses until her earnings reach about $23,000. ... She can almost make ends meet at about $19,000 in earnings, but by $20,000, her family is no longer eligible for food stamps and falls farther behind. If her earnings increase beyond $23,000, Becky will have a small cushion in her budget that could be used to cover an emergency. But if her income reaches $36,000, she will lose her child care subsidy. Subsequent earnings gains will be reduced as her children lose their health insurance, and Becky begins to pay premiums. Becky's earnings will have to increase to $40,000 before she breaks even again. The bottom line is that Becky's family is no better off financially if she earns $40,000 than if she earns $23,000.[26]

The work disincentives of the poverty trap spread throughout the bottom one-third of the workforce, those below 200 percent of the poverty line, which makes those work disincentives a big problem. But phasing out welfare benefits more slowly, reducing the effective marginal tax rate, would spread the remaining work disincentives (the whirlpool effect and the remaining poverty trap effective tax), and the dependency and spending burden of welfare, to higher and higher income levels. It would trap even middle-income families in welfare dependency.

The work disincentives created by welfare spread their devastating effects throughout entire low-income and minority communities, like a tornado growing in force. As more people in a poor neighborhood languish with little or no work, the entire local culture changes. Daily work is no longer the expected social norm. Extended periods of hanging around the neighborhood neither working nor going to school increasingly become socially acceptable, reinforcing the counterproductive incentive effects.

When productive activity makes no economic sense because of the work disincentives of welfare, counterproductive social activities proliferate. The resulting alcohol and drug abuse, recreational sex, out-of-wedlock births, and family break-up noted by Murray become the new social norms. Crime, a tax-free activity, becomes the natural outlet for more-enterprising, otherwise-idle, young men, spreading a culture of violence and ruining their future job prospects. The end result is the *culture of poverty*, a mutually reinforcing, downward-spiraling, vicious circle.

Family Break-Up and Out-of-Wedlock Births

Before the War on Poverty, black families generally remained intact and the overwhelming majority of black babies were born to two-parent families. Coinciding with the War on Poverty, however, the rate of out-of-wedlock births among black Americans soared from 28 percent in 1965, to 49 percent in 1975, 65 percent in 1990, and about 70 percent in 1995, where it remains today.[27]

Among white Americans, out-of-wedlock births soared from 4 percent in 1965, to 11 percent in 1980, 21 percent in 1990, and 25 percent in 1995, where it remains today. Among white high school dropouts, the rate of out-of-wedlock births is 48 percent. Among Americans overall, the rate of out-of-wedlock births has soared from 7 percent when the War on Poverty began to 39 percent today.

Out-of-wedlock births and single-parent families have negative effects on children. A vast body of research shows:

- Children from single-parent homes on average have lower educational achievement, perform poorly on standardized tests, and score lower on IQ tests than the overall population. In a study of nearly 14,000 children in grades 7–12 who had lived with at least one biological parent, those who experienced divorce, separation, or out-of-wedlock birth reported lower grade point averages than those who have always lived with both biological parents.[28]

- Children living in female-headed families with no spouse present had a poverty rate of 47.6 percent, more than four times the rate for married-couple families.[29] Nine percent of married families were living below the poverty level and 9 percent were receiving food stamps, compared with four times as many mother-only families who were living below poverty or receiving food stamps.[30]

- Seventy-one percent of high school dropouts live in homes where their father is not present. These children have more trouble academically, scoring poorly on tests of reading, mathematics, and thinking skills. Children from father-absent homes are less likely to attend school, more likely to be suspended or expelled from school, and more likely to drop out of school by age 16. After high school many of these children are also less likely to attain academic and professional qualifications.[31] They are 75 percent more likely to repeat a grade of school and 70 percent more likely to be expelled from school.

- Children from single-parent families are more likely to use drugs and are more than twice as likely to commit suicide.[32] Three of four teen suicides involve children whose fathers are absent from the home.

- Children from single-parent families are two to three times more likely to suffer from mental illness or other psychiatric disorders. Approximately 80 percent of children admitted to psychiatric hospitals come from single-parent homes.[33] These children are also more likely to exhibit behavioral problems such as hyperactivity, antisocial behavior, and anxiety. Children from single-parent homes represent 90 percent of runaways.

- A 2005 study of 1,409 rural southern adolescents (851 females and 558 males) aged 11–18 years investigated the statistical relationship between single-parent families and father absence and self-reported sexual activity. The study found adolescents in homes without fathers were more likely to report being sexually active when compared to adolescents living with their fathers.[34]

- Children raised by never-married mothers are 2.5 times more likely to be sexually active as teenagers. Males from single-parent homes are twice as likely to father a child out of wedlock. Females from fatherless homes are 111 percent more likely to have children as teenagers, 164 percent more likely to have a premarital birth, and 92 percent more likely to dissolve their own marriages.[35]

- A one-percentage-point increase in births to single mothers appears to increase the violent crime rate by approximately 1.7 percent.[36] A 2005 study in the *Journal of Marriage and Family*, using data from the National Longitudinal Study of Adolescent Health, found a 1 percent increase in the proportion of single-parent families in a neighborhood is associated with a 3 percent increase in an adolescent's level of violence.[37]

Studies show 72 percent of adolescent murderers, 70 percent of juvenile delinquents in state reform institutions, 60 percent of repeat rapists,[38] and most gang members come from single-parent homes.[39] Young black men raised in single-parent families are twice as likely as black men from two-parent families to commit crimes, and three times as likely if they come from a neighborhood with many single-parent families.[40] A seminal study published in the *Journal of Research in Crime and Delinquency* found a community's crime rate is more closely correlated with the percentage of single-parent families living there than with race or poverty.[41]

Out-of-wedlock births are the second key cause of poverty, in addition to non-work. For white, non-Hispanic female-headed households with children, the poverty rate increased to 33.1 percent in 2012 from 24.6 percent in 2000. The rate for black female-headed households with children also increased, moving up to 46.7 percent in 2012 from 41.0 percent in 2000. Hispanic female-headed households with children experienced an increase in poverty as well, moving to 48.6 percent in 2012 from 42.9 percent in 2000.[42]

Moreover, it is primarily these single-parent families that remain poor and dependent on welfare for the long term. Single-parent families perpetuate poverty into the next generation: Children raised in single-parent families are seven times more likely to become welfare recipients as adults. The negative effects on children from single-parent families, and the crime correlated with out-of-wedlock births, also perpetuate poverty long-term. As Rector explains, "If poor women who give birth outside of marriage were married to the fathers of their children, two-thirds would immediately be lifted out of poverty. Roughly 80 percent of all long-term poverty occurs in single-parent homes."[43]

Before enactment of national welfare reform – the Personal Responsibility and Work Opportunity Reconciliation Act of 1996 (PRWORA), described below – family break-up and out-of-wedlock births were the natural result of the incentives created by the country's massive, overgrown welfare empire. Having a baby was the gateway to a generous package of government benefits. Welfare made having children out of wedlock economically feasible. Besides costing taxpayers a fortune, welfare produced disastrous results among the low-income population, promoting the collapse of work and family, and perpetuating rather than ending poverty as a result.

Welfare Reform Begins

The Origins of Welfare Reform

The process of welfare reform began in California under Gov. Ronald Reagan, who was elected in 1966 and reelected in 1970 on a platform including reform of the welfare system. Shortly after his reelection, Reagan appointed his deputy director of the California Department of Public Works, a former career city manager named Robert Carleson, to be his director of the California Department of Social Welfare.[44] Carleson developed the first serious effort to reform the War on Poverty welfare programs.

Over the previous 10 years, the number of people on welfare in California had almost quadrupled from 600,000 to more than 2.2 million, and the available funds were spread so thin that benefit payments for the truly needy were inadequate.[45] The first reform goal was to restrict welfare benefits to those who were actually poor, the "truly needy," as Carleson called them.

Liberals had argued for phasing out welfare eligibility slowly as the income of the recipient rose, to reduce the disincentives and effective tax of the poverty trap on increasing work and income. But this had little impact in reducing the downward draft of welfare on the poor, because even those who were not truly needy could qualify for some assistance, which greatly increased costs for taxpayers and drew more people into the perverse disincentives of welfare. Reagan and Carleson reduced welfare rolls substantially first in California in the early 1970s, and then nationally in the early 1980s, by restricting welfare more tightly to those who were actually poor. At the same time, they increased benefits for the neediest.

Their second goal was "workfare," but this was more difficult to achieve. Reagan and Carleson wanted to require welfare recipients who could not find a private-sector job to work in community service for a number of hours each week sufficient to "earn" their benefits at an implicit wage rate roughly equivalent to the minimum wage. They reasoned requiring work for welfare would greatly reduce the non-work and family break-up incentives of welfare, as recipients would have to work regardless of their marital status.

Reagan and Carleson made some headway with workfare innovations in California, but federal law prevented them from adopting the full program. After Reagan became president (I worked directly for Carleson in the White House Office of Policy Development at the time), he and Carleson faced a roadblock in the Democrat-controlled House in getting the necessary changes in federal law to implement workfare nationwide. In 1987, Reagan finally won changes that would allow states to experiment with a broad range of work requirements and other welfare innovations, with a federally granted waiver of traditional program requirements.

Many conservatives did not expect the measure to be effective. But it helped spawn a welfare revolution in the states, with the most comprehensive and successful reforms achieved by Gov. Tommy Thompson in Wisconsin. Thompson essentially implemented the full workfare plan of Reagan and Carleson. The Thompson reformers were granted a waiver for the plan by President George H.W. Bush's Department of Health and Human Services, in probably the best domestic policy move of that entire administration.

The key to the Thompson reforms was a true work requirement for those on welfare, the first that had ever been fully implemented. Recipients who could not find private-sector jobs were required to do community-service work. If the recipient did not work the required hours, the family's AFDC and food stamp benefits were reduced proportionately. If the recipient did not work at all, the family would receive no AFDC or food stamp benefits.

Thompson added a further innovative component. To provide incentives for the state's welfare bureaucracy to fully and faithfully implement the reforms, funding for each local welfare office was dependent on the office's success in getting recipients to work. Local offices that proved unable to get recipients to work would be turned over to private contractors. With these incentives, the Wisconsin welfare bureaucracy implemented the reforms with startling efficiency and enthusiasm.

The results of the Thompson reforms were truly dramatic. The AFDC caseload in Wisconsin declined 81 percent. In the state outside Milwaukee, the caseload declined 95 percent. Even in inner-city Milwaukee, the number of welfare cases dropped 60 percent.

The Wisconsin reforms began to spread to other states across the country. Idaho and Wyoming achieved caseload reductions of 68 percent. Alabama, Mississippi, and New Mexico cut their caseloads in half. Nationwide, caseloads for the AFDC program dropped by one-fourth in the two-year period from September 1995 to September 1997.

Welfare Reform Goes National

By 1996, welfare reform was ready to go national. House Speaker Newt Gingrich (R-GA) and Rep. Clay Shaw (R-FL), chairman of the Welfare Subcommittee of the House Ways and Means Committee, led the reform effort to achieve the ultimate welfare reform goal of Reagan and Carleson: block grants to the states.[46] President Bill Clinton vetoed the reforms twice, but just before the 1996 elections he signed the bill, which the Republican Congress had passed for a third time.

The legislation focused on the Aid to Families with Dependent Children (AFDC) program, originally adopted in the 1930s as a central component of the New Deal. That program primarily paid cash to single mothers with children. Federal funding for the program was based on a matching formula: The more a state spent, the more money it received from the federal government. Most states received a federal dollar for each dollar they spent, but some received as much as four federal dollars for every state dollar, depending on average incomes in the state. This created new counterproductive incentives, effectively paying the states to spend more. And so they did, signing up increasing numbers of welfare recipients in good economic times and bad, thereby bringing more federal funds to their states. Those who tried to reduce welfare spending in their states, as Reagan did in California, were opposed because their reforms would mean the loss of federal funds.

Under the Personal Responsibility and Work Opportunity Reconciliation Act of 1996 (PRWORA), the share of federal spending on AFDC was returned to each state in a "block grant" to be used in a new program designed by the state based on mandatory work for the able-bodied. The grant is finite, not matching, so it does not vary with the amount the state spends. If the state wants to spend more than its federal block grant, it must pay for the extra spending itself. If the state spends less, it can keep the savings. This replaces the counterproductive incentives of the old system with positive incentives to weigh costs against benefits.

To give the states broad flexibility in designing the new program, the federal eligibility standards and benefit level requirements of the old AFDC program were repealed. That entailed repealing the entitlement status of AFDC, as states could not be free to redesign their programs if their citizens were entitled to coverage and benefits as specified in federal standards. States were explicitly authorized to use program funding for child care so parents could work, and for wage supplements for those who moved into private employment. The one remaining condition of federal funding was that the new state programs require work as a condition of receiving cash benefits. To reflect this new emphasis on work as opposed to extended dependency, the name of the program was changed to Temporary Assistance for Needy Families (TANF).

The liberal welfare establishment bitterly opposed the reforms. Their view was well-expressed by Sen. Daniel Patrick Moynihan (D-NY), the Urban Institute, and others who predicted the reforms would produce a "race to the bottom" among the states, and that within a year a million children would be starving in the streets.[47]

Quite to the contrary, the reform was remarkably successful,[48] exceeding even the predictions of its most ardent supporters. The old AFDC rolls were reduced by two-thirds nationwide, from a high of 14.2 million in 1993, the year before the state waiver experiments began to have an impact, to 4.6 million in 2006.[49] The rolls were reduced even more in states that pushed work most aggressively: Wyoming (97 percent), Idaho (90 percent), Florida (89 percent), Louisiana (89 percent), Illinois (89 percent), Georgia (89 percent), North Carolina (87 percent), Oklahoma (85 percent),

Wisconsin (84 percent), Texas (84 percent), and Mississippi (84 percent).[50] By 2006, the percent of the population receiving TANF cash welfare was down to 0.1 percent in Wyoming, 0.2 percent in Idaho, 0.5 percent in Florida, 0.6 percent in Georgia, Louisiana, North Carolina, and Oklahoma, and 0.7 percent in Arkansas, Colorado, Illinois, Nevada, Texas, and Wisconsin.[51]

In Illinois, former Fortune 1000 CEO Gary MacDougal chaired the Governor's Task Force on Human Services Reform, spearheading an overhaul of the state's welfare system. In *Make a Difference: A Spectacular Breakthrough in the Fight Against Poverty*, MacDougal notes between August 1996 and June 2003 the state's welfare rolls fell 86 percent. Even in Chicago's Cook County, welfare rolls fell 85 percent, with studies showing that most who left the rolls were working at pay above minimum wage.[52]

In his book evaluating the 1996 welfare reforms, *Work Over Welfare*, Ron Haskins of the Brookings Institution reports, "the number of families receiving cash welfare is now the lowest ... since 1969, and the percentage of children on welfare is lower than it has been since 1966."[53] The percentage of children on AFDC/TANF was reduced from 14.1 percent in 1994 to 4.7 percent in 2006.[54]

Not all adults left the AFDC/TANF rolls entirely. Among those who continued to receive some assistance from the program, more than 22 percent were working by 2006, up from 6.6 percent in 1988.[55]

Total federal and state spending on TANF by 2006 was nearly 10 percent below the 1995 peak in AFDC spending.[56] That reduction could and should have been much greater, given the reduction in caseloads. But political compromises in the original legislation limited both federal and state spending reductions. Nevertheless, in real inflation-adjusted dollars, total TANF spending by 2006 was down 31 percent from AFDC spending in 1995.[57]

Most importantly, total AFDC spending had increased 67 percent in just eight years from 1987 to 1995.[58] That means total spending on the program after reform was effectively reduced by close to half of what it would have been by 2006, 11 years later, under the old system at prior trends.

Child-care funding for low-income working parents has become a central component of the program, accounting for 19 percent of its expenditures.[59] That is further helping maximize work and minimize dependency. Haskins reports, "from 1993 to 2000 the portion of single mothers who were employed grew from 58% to nearly 75%, an increase of almost 30%," and "employment among never married mothers, most of whom join the welfare ranks within a year or two of giving birth, grew from 44% to 66%," an increase of 50 percent.[60] He adds, "Before 1996 never married mothers were the ones most likely to be school dropouts, to go on welfare, and to stay on welfare for a decade or more."[61]

Because of all this renewed work effort, the total income of low-income families formerly on welfare increased by about 25 percent over this period. Haskins reports,

> Between 1994 and 2000, child poverty fell every year and reached levels not seen since 1978. In addition, by 2000 the poverty rate of black children was the lowest it had ever been. The percentage of families in deep poverty, defined as half the poverty level, ... also declined until 2000, falling about 35% during the period.[62]

This decline in poverty "was widespread across demographic groups" and "the decline was caused by increased employment and earnings of female headed families."[63] Based on total income, poverty among these female-headed households declined by one-third, meaning nearly 4.2 million single mothers and children climbed out of poverty. Haskins cites a study by Isabel Sawhill of the Urban Institute and Paul Jargowsky, who conclude,

> So great was the decline in poverty that the number of neighborhoods with concentrated poverty fell precipitously, as did the number of neighborhoods classified as underclass because of the concentration of poverty and the high frequency of problems such as school dropout, female headed families, welfare dependency, and labor force dropout by adult males.[64]

The Child and Youth Well-Being Index, which tracks 28 key indicators of child well-being and is published annually by Ken Land of Duke University, increased by 30 percentage points from 1995 to 2005.[65]

Haskins concludes,

> The pattern is clear: earnings up, welfare down. This is the very definition of reducing welfare dependency. Most low income

mothers heading families appear to be financially better off because the mothers earn more money than they received from welfare. Taxpayers continue making a contribution to these families through the [Earned Income Tax Credit] and other work support programs, but the families earn a majority of their income. This explosion of employment and earnings constitutes an enormous achievement for the mothers themselves and for the nation's social policy.[66]

TANF is clearly better than AFDC was for the poor, as it draws them into work and out of poverty. It is better for taxpayers as well, saving huge sums, particularly as compared with what would have been spent had trends in AFDC spending continued.

Winning the War on Poverty: Block Grants for All

The 1996 welfare reform had one big shortcoming: It reformed only one program, AFDC. The federal government operates nearly 200 additional means-tested welfare programs, listed below.

Federal Means-Tested Programs
(186 plus programs)

Food and Nutrition Assistance
(13 programs)
Child and Adult Food Program
Child Nutrition
Child Nutrition Commodities
Commodity Supplemental Food Program
Emergency Food Assistance Program
Food Donations
Food Program Administration
Food Stamps
HHS: Congregate Meals
HHS: Meals on Wheels
Nutrition Assistance for Puerto Rico
Special Milk Program
Women, Infants and Children program

Social Services Programs
(34 programs)
Americorps: National Service Trust
Civilian Community Corps.
Community Development Block Grants
Community Economic Development

Community Food and Nutrition
Community Services Block Grants
Demonstration Partnership Agreements
Drug Education for Runaways
Emergency Food and Shelter (McKinney)
Emergency Community Services Grants
Farm Worker Assistance
Foster Grandparent Program
Juvenile Justice Discretionary Grants
Juvenile Justice Formula Grants (A&B)
Juvenile Monitoring (Part G)
Legal Services Corporation
National Youth Sports
Points of Light Foundation
Prevention Grants (Title V)
Retired Senior Volunteer Corps
Runaway and Homeless Youth
Rural Housing
Rural Community Facilities
Senior Companion Program
Senior Demonstrations
Service America

Social Services Block Grant
Special Volunteers programs
State Challenge Grants (Part E)
Transition Living for Homeless Youth
VISTA
VISTA - Literary
Youth Community Corps.
Youth Gangs (Part D)

Low Income Housing Programs
(27 programs)
Bureau of Indian Affairs Housing Grants
Emergency Shelter Grants to Homeless
Farm Labor Housing Grants
Farm Labor Housing Loans
Home Investment Partnership Program
    (HOME)
Homeownership and Opportunity for People
    Everywhere (HOPE)
Housing Opportunities for Persons with AFDC
Innovative Homeless Initiatives Demonstration
Low Income Home Energy Assistance Program
    (LIHEAP)
Project Based Rental Assistance
Public Housing Section 236
Rural Rental Housing Grants
Rural Housing Repair Grants
Rural Housing Repair Loans
Rural Rental Housing Grants
Rural Self-Help Housing TA Grants
Section 8
Section 8 Moderate Rehab for SROs
Section 101 Rent Supplements
Section 202 Elderly
Section 235 Homeownership Assistance
Section 502 Rural Home Loans
Section 521 Rural Rental Assistance
Section 523 Self-Help Housing Site Loans
Section 524 Rural Housing Site Loans
Section 533 Rural Housing Preservation Grants
Section 811 Disabled
Shelter Plus Care
Supportive Housing for Homeless

Health Programs for Low Income People
(23 programs)
Adolescent Family Life Demonstration Grants
CARE Grant Program
Centers of Excellence
Community Health Centers
Education Assistance Regarding
    Undergraduates

Family Planning Program
Health Care Services for Homeless
Health Services for Residents of Public
    Housing
Healthy Start Initiative
Immunization Program
Indian Health Services
Maternal and Child Health Block Grant
Medicaid
Migrant Health Centers
National Health Service Corps Field Program
National Health Service Corps Recruitment
    Program
Nurse Education Opportunities
Projects for Assistance in Transition and
    Homelessness
Rural Health Services Outreach Grants
Scholarships for Disadvantaged Student
    Faculty
Setaside for Community Integrated Services
    Systems
Setaside for Special Projects of National
    Significance
Vaccines for Children

Federal Employment and Training
Programs for Low Income People
(31 programs)
Adult Education - State Administered Basic
    Grant Programs
All Volunteer Force Educational Assistance
Economic Development Grants for Public
    Works and Development
Employment Service - Wagner Peyser State
    Grants
Federal Pell Grant
Federal Supplemental Education Opportunity
    Grants
Food Stamp Employment & Training
Guaranteed Student Loans
Job Opportunities and Basic Skills Program
JTPA EDWAA -Dislocated Workers
    (Governor's Discretionary)
JTPA EDWAA -Dislocated Workers
    (Secretary's Discretionary)
JTPA EDWAA - Dislocated Workers (Substate
    Allotment)
JTPA IIA Training Services for the
    Disadvantaged—Adult
JTPA IIB Training Services for Disadvantaged
    Summer Youth
JTPA IIB Training Services for Employment

and Training Program
JTPA IIC Disadvantaged Youth
JTPA Job Corps
Miscellaneous (93 programs with spending less than $100 million, 31 programs authorized but with no appropriation)
One Stop Career Centers
Rehab Services Basic Support Grants to States
School to Work
Senior Community Service Employment Program
State Legalization Impact Assistance Grants
Student Support Services
Supportive Housing Demonstration Program
Survivors and Dependents Educational Assistance
Trade Adjustment Assistance - Workers
Upward Bound
Vocational Education - Basic State Programs
Vocational Education - Tech Prep Education
Vocational Rehab for Disabled Veterans

Federal Child Care Programs for Low Income Families (24 Programs)
Abandoned Infants Assistance Act
Appalachian Childhood Development
At Risk Child Care
Child Care and Development Block Grant
Child Care for Recipients of AFDC
Child Care Licensing Improvement Grants
Child Welfare Services
Comprehensive Child Development Centers
Early Childhood Development Program
Early Intervention Grants for Infants and Families
Employer Provided Child or Dependent Care Services
Family Self-Sufficiency Program
Homeless Supportive Housing Program
Migrant and Seasonal Farmworkers Programs
Native Hawaiian Family Education Centers
Residential Substance Abuse Treatment for Women
Special Child Care Services for Disadvantaged College Students
Special Education Preschool Grants
State Dependent Care Planning and Development Grants
Substance Abuse Prevention and Treatment Block Grant
Summer Youth Employment and Training Program

Temporary Child Care for Children with Disabilities and Crisis Nurseries
Transitional Child Care
Youth Training Program

Federal Child Welfare and Child Abuse Programs for Low Income Families (28 programs)
Abandoned Infants Assistance
Adoption Opportunities Program
Child Abuse Demonstration and Research Grants
Child Abuse State Grant Program
Children's Advocacy Centers
Children's Justice Grant Program'
Child Welfare Research and Demonstration
Child Welfare Services
Child Welfare Training
Community Based Family Resource Program
Crisis Nurseries program
Demonstration Grants for Abuse of Homeless Children
Entitlement for Adoption (4 programs)
Entitlement for Foster Care (3 programs)
Family Preservation and Family Support Program
Family Unification Program
Family Violence State Grant Program
Family Support Centers
Grants to improve the investigation and prosecution of child abuse cases
Independent Living
Missing and Exploited Children's Program
Temporary Child Care for Children with Disabilities
Treatment for juvenile offenders who are victims of child abuse and neglect

Federal Education Programs for Low Income Families (4 programs)
Even Start
Head Start
Migrant Education
Title I Education for the Disadvantaged

Cash Assistance (3 programs)
Low Income Home Energy Assistance Program (LIHEAP)
Supplemental Security Income Program (SSI)
Temporary Assistance for Needy Families (TANF)

Ideally, all of the programs listed here would be block-granted to the states, not individually but in one lump sum, with the states free to use the money for assistance to the poor as they each deem best and most effective. Practically, this would involve a number of separate bills, coordinated to work together. One would reform Medicaid, big enough for its own bill, probably along with SCHIP. Other programs would be grouped in their own bills, perhaps as shown in the categories above. But the federal funding for each would be provided through finite block grants, not with matching federal funding formulas giving more money to each state the more the state spends. To the extent the state spends more on its new, redesigned, welfare system, the state would pay for it out of the pockets of its own taxpayers. To the extent the state spends less, it can keep the money for other uses.

Block-granting the remaining means-tested welfare programs would effectively amount to sending welfare back to the states, with continued federal assistance in financing. As Carleson wrote,

Until President Lyndon Johnson sought to establish his Great Society, welfare in America was primarily a state, local, and private responsibility. Federal spending was modest. But following Washington's takeover of welfare during the 1960s War on Poverty, government welfare spending soared.[67]

With the states back in charge, each would have the flexibility to structure its welfare system to suit the needs and circumstances of its citizens. The administrative savings alone would be substantial. State control also would allow experimentation among the states, with real-world results proving what works and what doesn't. Economic and political competition among the states would lead them to adopt what has proven to work best.

Such block-grant reforms would achieve the ultimate dream of Reagan and Carleson in restoring the original federalism and state control over welfare. It also follows the spirit of the new Tea Party movement across the country in restoring power to the states and reining in government spending, deficits, and debt. And it would be much more efficient and effective at achieving the stated goals of sincere welfare-state proponents, as the reform would benefit the poor through increased work and the resulting increased incomes. Indeed, as discussed below, the reform offers the prospect of completely eliminating poverty in America.

As noted earlier, the best estimate of the total current cost of these nearly 200 means-tested welfare programs is $10.3 trillion for the years 2009 to 2018.[68] Granting there are significant differences among these 200 programs and the results will not be the same for each, I nevertheless contend the resulting savings would be on par overall with the savings achieved by the 1996 AFDC reforms: The net cost to the taxpayers would be reduced by half, with a savings of $5 trillion over 10 years.

The federal funding for these programs should be apportioned among the states in accordance with current federal funding formulas to the extent possible. Those formulas reflect political compromises already reached, and the reform would be endangered by reopening this most political of all battles. Federal requirements on the use of these funds by the states should be limited to just three. First, they must be used to assist poor and low-income families. Second, they must be used without discrimination in accordance with federal civil rights laws. Third, the assistance must be provided in return for work, except in the case of the disabled or retired seniors who should no longer be expected to work.

The Fundamental Importance of Work

As Carleson advises, "Assistance could only be provided in return for work from the able-bodied adults in the family, and the states would be free to carry this out."[69] He further explains, "Able-bodied people must work first in order to receive any welfare benefit; benefits will be earned before the money flows."[70]

Carleson's advice shows how the reform could entirely eliminate poverty in the United States. That is because already under current law – for anyone who works full-time in the United States – the minimum wage, augmented by the Earned Income Tax Credit plus the Child Tax Credit, equals or exceeds the poverty level for every possible family combination, including single persons with or without children:

- For a single person working full-time, (40 hours per week) at the current federal minimum wage of $7.25 an hour, annual earnings equal $15,080 a year (40 hours per week x 52 weeks = 2,080 hours @ $7.25 = $15,080). In addition, that person qualifies for an Earned Income Tax Credit in 2014 of $496, for a total income for the year of $15,576, exceeding the federal poverty level for 2014, which for a single person living alone is $11,670.

- For a single person working full-time with one child, the Earned Income Tax Credit increases for 2014 to $3,305. The family would receive an additional $1,000 per year from the Child Tax Credit. Adding income from full-time work at the minimum wage equals a total for the year of $19,385 in income, well above the poverty level for 2014 for a single person with a child: $15,730.

- With two children, the Earned Income Tax Credit for 2014 increases to $5,460, and the Child Tax Credit to $2,000. With $15,080 from full-time work at the minimum wage, that totals $22,540 in annual income, while the poverty level for 2014 for a single person with two children is $19,790.

- With three children, the Earned Income Tax Credit for 2014 increases to $6,143, and the Child Tax Credit to $3,000. With full-time work at the minimum wage, family income would total $24,223, while the federal poverty level for 2014 for a single person with three children is $23,850.

The real escape from poverty is tied to intact families. When fathers "stick around," work full-time, and contribute to the welfare of their children, that adds at least another $15,080 a year to the family's income level. That is why there is no poverty at all among two-parent families when both parents are working full-time.

If States Were in Control

How should states redesign their welfare systems to take advantage of their newfound control over the block-granted funds? State officials must focus on incentives. All the perverse, counterproductive incentives for non-work, family breakup, and out-of-wedlock child-bearing should be eliminated and replaced with positive, pro-growth incentives for work, savings, investment, entrepreneurship, prosperity, and marriage before childbearing.

They should rely on modern labor markets as much as possible to provide essential income support for the poor and lower-income families. That in turn would minimize the burden on taxpayers for meeting the basic needs of poor and low-income families. With incentives to inspire the low-income population to work, that population would contribute in a meaningful way to a booming economy.

Moreover, when the able-bodied are required to work to receive benefits, the incentives switch to favor marriage before childbearing. Every man and woman would know someone will have to work to support every child. Bearing a child would no longer result in free benefits. That eliminates any incentive for childbearing out of wedlock and creates powerful incentives for marriage first, so there will be a husband and father, as well as wife and mother, who can help share the responsibility for work to support the child and the family.

Work Opportunities for All

Exactly how to implement an effective work requirement would be left up to each state. But if I were helping state officials redesign their welfare programs, I would encourage them to require the able-bodied to show up for work *first*, before receiving any benefits, embodying the original Reagan concept of workfare.

Those who reported to their local welfare office before 9 a.m. would be guaranteed a work assignment paying the minimum wage in cash for an eight-hour-day's work. A private job assignment would be the top priority, but if one were not available that day, the applicant would be assigned to some government-directed activity serving the community. The worker would be paid in cash at the end of the day. Those who needed more money would come back for work again the next day.

The government would provide free daycare for the young children of adults who desired it. Medicaid-financed doctors would be available at the daycare facilities to examine and treat the children if necessary and desired.

For the adults who report for work regularly, the welfare office would find them a private job assignment, just as for-profit temp agencies do in the private sector. Indeed, local welfare offices could be contracted out to private agencies, especially if the local welfare bureaucracy proves unsuccessful in finding private-sector jobs for the poor in need.

Organizing local employers to offer jobs would be a function for the welfare administrators and private charitable efforts. In some prosperous local economies, employers can be ready and available to absorb everyone who shows up needing work. Organizing that can be a function of local Chambers of Commerce and other business groups, as well as church organizations. The more people and groups involved in this, the better for everyone. Such a system would promote real social solidarity.

Those who work a minimum number of hours each month would get a

Medicaid voucher sufficient to purchase basic private health insurance. Those who work for a continued period establishing a regular work history would be eligible for help in purchasing a home.

The state could choose to provide additional assistance for transportation if it deems that desirable. It could even provide assistance for education and training. But that should not be allowed to become an excuse for extended nonwork.

This guaranteed offer of work would produce much better results than the old workfare model, where benefits calculated under some government formula are paid first and then the bureaucrats chase after the beneficiaries to make them work a sufficient number of hours to work off the benefit at the minimum wage. Once the benefits are already paid, the recipients have no incentive to work, and they come up with endless imaginative excuses as to why they cannot. Penalties to enforce the work requirement become socially difficult to enforce and are too easily characterized as cruel impositions on needy people.

With work first and payment later in return, this intractable situation is reversed. The beneficiaries have every incentive to work and will be eager to do so, without penalty or enforced requirement. If they decide not to work, that is their choice. The taxpayers lose nothing as a result. Of course, low-income parents are under the same legal obligation to provide for their children as everyone else. If they fail to do so, with a guaranteed offer of work always waiting for them, that is actionable neglect.

How Work Can Change Culture

Consider how this proposal would reverse the perverse incentives of the current welfare system into incentives for positive, productive actions. The incentives for family breakup and out-of-wedlock childbearing would be eliminated. If the mother has a child without a husband, she must go to work to support the child. Even the Child Tax Credit can and should be tied to work, as the EITC is.

Moreover, there is nothing to be gained under this system by avoiding marriage or by couples splitting up. No benefits are provided to the mother for being unmarried. A government welfare check does not become a substitute for a working husband. If the father must work to support himself anyway and will be charged for child support, he has no economic incentive to stay away from the family.

To the contrary, since living together will reduce living expenses the couple will have to work to pay for, the incentives are for family unification rather than family breakup. Couples staying together can help each other by sharing the necessary work if they desire. A single mother could avoid work altogether by marrying a working husband. Thus the system provides reinforcing economic incentives for marriage. Alternatively, a single mother may return to live with her own parents to reduce living expenses and the need to work to pay for them. This is another form of family reunification that also reduces the dependency burden on taxpayers.

The incentives for nonwork are reversed as well. There is nothing to be gained under this system by not working. No benefits are given to those who choose not to work. There is no whirlpool work disincentive as discussed above. Rather, the incentive is to take whatever private-sector job is available, since the able-bodied will have to work to support themselves in any event, and in the private sector the worker will gain skills, raises, promotions, and new opportunities over time. Instead of taxpayers paying the bottom 20 percent of income earners a trillion dollars a year not to work, employers would be paying them much more to work.

The resulting incentives would reduce dependency, and the burden on taxpayers, in other ways as well. Under the current welfare system, working at modest-income jobs makes a man economically harmful to his low-income family, and the welfare benefits become an economic substitute for husbands. Not surprisingly, young men in low-income communities lose interest in work. But under the new system, working makes a man more desirable to the opposite sex, as he becomes a means for a woman to avoid otherwise necessary work.

Together, these incentive effects change culture. Everybody in the neighborhood, except maybe women supported by working men, is now going to work. That becomes reestablished as the social norm. Having babies without husbands, and family breakup, will be recognized by everyone as costly practices not to be emulated. Bearing children only after marriage will be recognized as the smart practice. These new cultural realities will further encourage socially productive choices and actions.

Reduced illegitimacy and family breakup produced by the changed incentives will result in far less social need. The resulting transformation of the cultural environment would reinforce these positive effects. The new system would cost only a fraction of the current system, ultimately saving trillions of dollars over the years while breaking the poor out of the poverty trap.

Conclusion

These reforms ultimately work because, as Charles Murray and Robert Rector have shown, we are already spending far more than enough to eliminate poverty in America. Replacing the enormously counterproductive incentives of the current system with productive incentives that inspire the lower-income population to work and to establish and maintain intact families would result in enormous savings to taxpayers as compared with the current system, while enabling us to eliminate poverty in the United States.

Some on the political Left may complain the poor will be deprived of dignity if they must work to feed, clothe, and shelter themselves and their families. The great majority of Americans will not share this perverse moral view. It is living at the expense of others when you are perfectly capable of providing for yourself that is undignified.

Moreover, the policies advocated here would simply give states the power to choose. If they want to adopt state-level versions of the current failed national policies, they would be free to make that choice. Maybe that is what California, Massachusetts, and New York will choose. Or maybe this new freedom to choose would stimulate political revolutions in those states as well.

The reform proposed here also would promote economic growth. Instead of taxpayers paying the bottom 20 percent of the income ladder a trillion dollars a year not to work, private employers would be paying them more, to work. That increased labor flowing into the economy would join the increased capital flowing into the economy from personal Social Security accounts discussed in Chapter 2. The result would be a powerful, transformative boost to economic growth and prosperity, especially for the poorest 20 percent.

In addition, with incomes for the poor coming from work rather than government payments for broken families, the welfare incentives for family break-up would be eliminated. Those perverse incentives would be replaced instead with incentives for family formation and maintenance, so parents could share the necessary work and child care and child-raising responsibilities.

This reform would end the poverty trap and free the nation's poor to become productive citizens and raise children prepared for lives better than their parents had.

Notes

1. Congressional Budget Office, *The Budget and Economic Outlook: Fiscal Years 2011 to 2021*, January 2011, p. 62.

2. U.S. Department of Agriculture, http://www.fns.usda.gov/pd/34snapmonthly.htm.

3. Robert Rector, Katherine Bradley, and Rachel Sheffield, *Obama to Spend $10.3 Trillion on Welfare: Uncovering the Full Cost of Means-Tested Welfare or Aid to the Poor* (Washington, DC: The Heritage Foundation, 2009).

4. *Ibid.*, pp. 15–16.

5. Charles Murray, *In Our Hands: A Plan to Replace the Welfare State* (Washington, DC: American Enterprise Institute, 2006).

6. Rector *et al.*, *supra* note 3, p. 2.

7. Edgar K. Browning, *Stealing from Each Other: How the Welfare State Robs Americans of Money and Spirit* (London, UK: Praeger, 2008).

8. Rector *et al.*, *supra* note 3, p. 11.

9. *Ibid.*, p. 12.

10. *Ibid.* The amount specifically is $15.92 trillion.

11. *Ibid.*

12. *Ibid.*, p. 13.

13. *Ibid.*, pp. 7–8.

14. Robert Rector, "How Poor Are America's Poor?" Heritage Foundation *Backgrounder* No. 2064, The Heritage Foundation, August 27, 2007.

15. *Ibid.*, p. 3.

16. U.S. Bureau of the Census, *Current Population Reports*, Series P-60, No. 80, Income in 1970 of Families and Persons in the United States, p. 26.

17. U.S. Bureau of the Census, *Current Population Reports*, Series P-60, No. 180, Money Income of Households, Families, and Persons in the United States: 1991, p. 7.

18. SRI International, *Final Report of the Seattle-Denver Income Maintenance Experiment, Vol. I, Design and Results* (Washington, DC: February 25, 1991).

19. Arthur B. Laffer and Stephen Moore, *Return to Prosperity* (New York, NY: Simon and Schuster, 2010), Chapter 19.

20. *Ibid.*, pp. 211–212.

21. Arthur B. Laffer, "The Tightening Grip of the Poverty Trap," A.B. Laffer Associates, April 29, 1983.

22. Laffer and Moore, *supra* note 19, p. 212.

23. Linda Ginnarelli and Eugene Steuerle, "The Twice Poverty Trap: Tax Rates Faced by AFDC Recipients," Urban Institute, 1996.

24. *Ibid.*

25. Jeff Frankel, "Effective Marginal Tax Rates on Lower Income American Workers," February 8, 2008, http://content.ksg.harvard.edu/blog/jeff_frankels_weblog/2008/02/08/8/.

26. Nancy K. Cauthen, "When Work Doesn't Pay: What Every Policymaker Should Know," National Center for Children in Poverty, June 2006 (as quoted by Laffer and Moore, *supra* note 19, pp. 214–215).

27. The rate is officially reported by the National Center for Health Statistics. See also Jason L. Riley, "The State Against Blacks: The Weekend Interview with Walter Williams," *The Wall Street Journal*, January 22–23, 2011, p. A13.

28. K.H. Tillman, "Family Structure Pathways and Academic Disadvantage among Adolescents in Stepfamilies," *Sociological Inquiry*, Vol. 77, no. 3 (August 2007): 383–424, http://onlinelibrary.wiley.com/doi/10.1111/j.1475-682X.2007.00198.x/pdf.

29. Office of the Assistant Secretary for Planning and Evaluation, U.S. Department of Health & Human Services, "Information on Poverty and Income Statistics: A Summary of 2012 Current Population Survey Data," *ASPE Issue Brief,* September 12, 2012, http://aspe.hhs.gov/hsp/12/PovertyAndIncomeEst/ib.cfm.

30. Jonathan Vespa, Jamie M. Lewis, and Rose M. Kreider, *America's Families and Living Arrangements: 2012*, United States Census Bureau, August 2013, http://www.census.gov/prod/2013pubs/p20-570.pdf.

31. Edward Kruk, Ph.D., "The Vital Importance of Paternal Presence in Children's Lives," May 23, 2012. http://www.psychologytoday.com/blog/co-parenting-after-divorce/201205/father-absence-father-deficit-father-hunger.

32. J. Bronte-Tinkew, K.A. Moore, R.C. Capps, and J. Zaff, "The Influence of Father Involvement On Youth Risk Behaviors among Adolescents: a Comparison of Native Born and Immigrant Families," *Social Science Research,* Vol. 35 (2006): 181–209, http://www.sciencedirect.com/science/article/pii/S0049089X04000845.

33. Jack Block, *et al.*, "Parental Functioning and the Home Environment in Families of Divorce," *Journal of the American Academy of Child and Adolescent Psychiatry*, Vol. 27 (1988), http://www.sciencedirect.com/science/article/pii/S0890856709655519.

34. C.S. Hendricks, S.K. Cesario, C. Murdaugh, M.E. Gibbons, E.J. Servonsky, R.V. Bobadilla, D.L. Hendricks, B. Spencer-Morgan, and A. Tavakoli, "The Influence of Father Absence on the Self-esteem and Self-reported Sexual Activity of Rural Southern Adolescents," *The ABNF Journal*, Vol. 16, no. 6 (Nov–Dec 2005): 124–31, http://www.academia.edu/4660574/The_Influence_of_Father_Absence_on_the_Self-Esteem_and_Self-Reported_Sexual_Activity_of_Rural_Southern_Adolescents.

35. R. Maginnis, "Challenges to Children's Well Being: Fathers and Parental Time" Remarks to The World Congress of Families II, http://worldcongress.org/wcf2_spkrs/wcf2_maginnis.htm.

36. *Ibid.*

37. C. Knoester and D.A. Hayne, "Community Context, Social Integration into Family, and Youth Violence," *Journal of Marriage and Family*, Vol. 67, no. 3 (August 2005): 767–780, http://onlinelibrary.wiley.com/doi/10.1111/j.1741-3737.2005.00168.x/abstract.

38. Raymond A. Knight and Robert A. Prentky, "The Developmental Antecedents and Adult Adaptations of Rapist Subtypes," *Criminal Justice and Behavior*, vol. 14, no. 4 (December 1987), pp. 403–426, http://cjb.sagepub.com/content/14/4/403.short.

39. See Nicholas Davidson, "Life Without Father," *Policy Review*, Winter 1990; and Karl Zinsmeister, "Growing Up Scared," *The Atlantic*, June 1990.

40. Anne Hill and June O'Neill, "Underclass Behaviors in the United States: Measurement and Analysis of Determinants," Center for the Study of Business and Government, Baruch College, February 1992.

41. Douglas Smith and G. Roger Jarjoura, "Social Structure and Criminal Victimization," *Journal of Research in Crime and Delinquency*, February 1988, pp. 27–56, http://jrc.sagepub.com/content/25/1/27.abstract.

42. Joan Entmacher, Katherine Gallagher Robbins, Julie Vogtman, and Lauren Frohlich, *Insecure & Unequal: Poverty and Income among Women and Families 2000–2012*, National Women's Law Center, 2013, http://www.nwlc.org/sites/default/files/pdfs/final_2013_nwlc_povertyreport.pdf.

43. Rector *et al.*, *supra* note 3, p. 25.

44. Susan A. Carleson and Hans A. Zeiger, *Government Is the Problem: Memoirs of Ronald Reagan's Welfare Reformer* (Alexandria, VA: American Civil Rights Union, 2009), pp. 4, 15.

45. *Ibid.*, pp. xix, xx.

46. *Ibid.*, pp. 104–105.

47. *Ibid.*, pp. 138–139.

48. Gary MacDougal, Kate Campaigne, and Dane Wendell, "Welfare Reform after Ten Years: A State-by-State Analysis," *Report Card*, The Heartland Institute, June 2008.

49. U.S. House of Representatives, Ways and Means Committee, *The 2008 Green Book*, Section 7, Temporary Assistance for Needy Families, Table 7-8, pp. 7–27; see also *Ibid.*

50. *The 2008 Green Book, ibid.*, Table 7-9, pp. 7-28—7-29.

51. *Ibid.*

52. Gary MacDougal, *Make a Difference: A Spectacular Breakthrough in the Fight Against Poverty* (New York, NY: St. Martin's Griffin Truman Talley Books, 2005).

53. Ron Haskins, *Work Over Welfare: The Inside Story of the 1996 Welfare Reform Law* (Washington, DC: Brookings Institution, 2006), p. 334.

54. *The 2008 Green Book*, *supra* note 49, p. 7-26.

55. *Ibid.*, p. 7-54.

56. *Ibid.*, Table 7-4, pp. 7-13—7-14.

57. *Ibid.*

58. *Ibid.*

59. *Ibid.*, p. 7-17.

60. Haskins, *supra* note 53, p. 335.

61. *Ibid.*

62. *Ibid.*, p. 336.

63. *Ibid.*

64. *Ibid.*, p. 337.

65. Kenneth Land, "Child and Youth Well-Being Index (CWI), 1975–2004 with Projections for 2005," Department of Sociology, Duke University, www.soc.duke.edu/~cwi/.

66. Haskins, *supra* note 53, p. 335.

67. Carleson and Zeiger, *supra* note 44, p. 107.

68. Rector *et al.*, *supra* note 3.

69. Carleson and Zeiger, *supra* note 44, p. 112.

70. *Ibid.*, p. 124.

5

Liberating the Poor from the Medicaid Ghetto

Medicaid is the national entitlement program for the poor meant to ensure no individual is deprived of essential health care benefits because of his or her socioeconomic standing. It is also a central component of the entitlement crisis threatening to bankrupt the nation.

Skyrocketing Costs, But Still Poor Health Care

Financing for Medicaid is shared with the states under a federal formula, with the federal government paying about 60 percent of the costs on average. Federal Medicaid costs are growing under President Barack Obama, increasing rapidly since the passage of Obamacare.

Federal spending on Medicaid was $200 billion in 2008, President George W. Bush's last year in office. The Obama administration's own budget projections estimate federal Medicaid spending will skyrocket to close to three times its 2008 level by 2024, reaching $552 billion.[1] From the time Obamacare went into effect in 2014 until 2024, federal spending for the program is expected to total $4.65 trillion.[2]

In addition to that massive federal tax burden, Medicaid will cost state governments another $3.07 trillion. The National Association of State Budget Officers reported states already spend more on Medicaid than anything else, even K–12 education programs.[3] The Centers for Medicare and Medicaid Services (CMS) projected total federal and state costs for Medicaid will reach more than $853.6 billion by 2022.[4] The program will be on track to cost more than a trillion dollars one year later. Between 2013 and 2022, federal and state government spending for Medicaid will total

$6.56 trillion, according to CMS estimates.

As a result of Obamacare, the Congressional Budget Office (CBO) predicted 85 million Americans would enroll in Medicaid, increasing the total number of recipients to nearly 100 million by 2021, up from 47.7 million in 2008 and 54.6 million at the time of Obamacare's adoption in 2010.[5] The influx of program beneficiaries is contributing to the rapidly rising costs of the program.

Despite the program's enormous overhead, Medicaid forces doctors and hospitals to shoulder 40 percent or more of treatment costs. Consequently, Medicaid patients face difficulties in obtaining timely, essential health care, suffering from adverse health as a result. Scott Gottlieb of the New York University School of Medicine noted in a March 10, 2011 commentary in *The Wall Street Journal* ("Medicaid Is Worse Than No Coverage at All"), "In some states, they've cut reimbursements to providers so low that beneficiaries can't find doctors willing to accept Medicaid."[6]

Gottlieb explained, "Dozens of recent medical studies show that Medicaid patients suffer for it. In some cases, they'd do just as well without health insurance" as a result of their limited access to physicians. He reported a 2010 study of throat cancer "found that Medicaid patients and people lacking any health insurance were both 50 percent more likely to die when compared with privately insured patients."[7]

Similarly, a 2011 study of heart patients "found that people with Medicaid who underwent coronary angioplasty were 59 percent more likely to have ... strokes and heart attacks, compared with privately insured patients. Medicaid patients were also more than twice as likely to have a major, subsequent heart attack after angioplasty as were patients who didn't have any health insurance at all."[8] A 2010 analysis of major surgical procedures "found that being on Medicaid was associated with the longest length of stay, the most total hospital costs, and the highest risk of death."[9]

Gottlieb noted, "In all of these studies, the researchers controlled for the socioeconomic and cultural factors that can negatively influence the health of poorer patients on Medicaid."[10] The problem was that "payment to providers ha[d] been reduced to literally pennies on each dollar of customary charges,"[11] compromising the ability of severely ill Medicaid patients to gain timely access to essential specialists.

The problem is illustrated in the case of a Maryland boy, 12-year-old Deamonte Driver.[12] When Deamonte complained of a toothache, his mother tried to find a dentist who would take Medicaid, but only 900 of 5,500 dentists in Maryland accept the program's beneficiaries. By the time she found one and scheduled an appointment for the boy, his tooth had abscessed and the infection had spread to his brain. Because of the delay, she had to find a brain specialist who accepted Medicaid. Before she could find one, the boy was rushed to Children's Hospital for emergency surgery. He called his mother from his hospital room one night to say, "Make sure you pray before you go to sleep." In the morning, he was dead.

Freedom Under Block Grants

The unwillingness of health care providers to accept Medicaid patients because of the program's shamefully low reimbursement rates could be addressed by extending to Medicaid the 1996 reforms of the Aid to Families with Dependent Children (AFDC) program. That reform returned a share of federal spending on AFDC to each state in the form of a "block grant" for use in new welfare programs redesigned by state governments.

As Medicaid is now, federal funding for AFDC originally was based on a matching formula, with the federal government giving more to each state the more it spent on the program. The 1996 reform made the block grants to each state finite; federal funding did not vary with the amount the state spent. If a state's revamped welfare program cost more, the state had to pay the extra costs itself. If the program cost less, the state could keep the savings.

State bureaucrats administering the block-granted welfare program thus had an incentive to shrink rather than grow their welfare rolls. The old AFDC rolls were reduced by two-thirds nationwide and even more in states that most aggressively required beneficiaries to work, as recipients formerly on the program went to work or married an individual who worked.[13] The incomes of these former AFDC dependents were documented to have increased by 25 percent as a result.[14] Total federal and state spending on the program by 2006 was down by 31 percent in real dollars from AFDC spending in 1995, more than half of what it would have been based on prior trends.[15]

These reforms should be extended to Medicaid, replacing the federal matching formula with fixed, finite block grants. Each state would be free to use the funds for its own redesigned health care safety net program for the poor in return for work from the able-bodied.

Rhode Island offers an example of how the block-granting reform would work. It received a broad waiver from federal Medicaid requirements in return for a fixed cap on federal financing for five years. The state turned to managed care, competitive bidding by health care providers, and comprehensive case management by private insurers for those on Medicaid. It shifted long-term care out of nursing homes to home- and community-based care.

The Lewin Group, a health care consulting firm, studied Rhode Island's reforms and concluded they were "highly effective in controlling Medicaid costs" while improving "access to more appropriate services." The state's costs were reduced by nearly 30 percent in the first 18 months alone, and the poor were assigned health providers to ensure they received essential care.[16]

Alternatively, states could serve the poor by using the program to provide vouchers that would help pay for the private health insurance of their choice in the competitive marketplace. Health insurance vouchers would free the poor from the Medicaid ghetto, enabling them to obtain the same health care as middle-income families.

States would have the authority to establish health savings accounts (HSAs) for the poor, which maximize consumer choice over their own health care and consumer control over the funds. Such HSAs, backed up with catastrophic health insurance for high-cost medical necessities, provide powerful, effective incentives for consumers themselves to decide how to reduce costs and preserve maximum funds for the future.[17]

Any of these options would positively affect the ability of Medicaid recipients to receive essential care. Because the program currently pays doctors and hospitals so poorly, Medicaid is essentially an institutionalized mechanism for denying health care to the poor. Reform would mean much better access to essential health care for the poor and their families when it is needed.

Just as the 1996 block grants for AFDC provided significant savings for taxpayers while serving the poor more effectively, so too would block grants save Medicaid. This reform proposal was included in the federal budgets proposed by then-House Budget Committee Chairman Paul Ryan (R-WI), which were adopted by the full House. CBO estimated such block grants would save federal taxpayers nearly a trillion dollars over 10 years.

The State Health Flexibility Act, cosponsored by Reps. Paul Broun (R-GA), Tim Huelskamp (R-KS), Jim Jordan (R-OH) (former head of the House Republican Study Committee), and Todd Rokita (R-IN), is a more aggressive solution. The bill has stricter limits on federal Medicaid funding over time, and CBO scored it to save nearly $2 trillion over 10 years.

Such Medicaid block-grant bills would have to start with the repeal of Obamacare's Medicaid expansion, similar to the repeal and replacement of Obamacare itself, discussed in Chapter 6. About half the states enacted the Medicaid expansion provided for under Obamacare, while half did not.

Simply block-granting current, post-Obamacare federal financing of Medicaid would reward those states that have chosen to expand Medicaid under Obamacare at the expense of states that have not. Replacing Obamacare will assure health care for all with enhanced benefits for the poor.

Under the Medicaid block-grant proposal advocated here, states would each be free to expand the program. But they would have to accomplish that expansion entirely with their own funds.

The State Children's Health Insurance Program (SCHIP), which pays for health insurance for children from modest-income families that earn too much to qualify for Medicaid, should be rolled into the Medicaid block grants as well. Those children can then be served by the new state programs, which would provide better health care under the health insurance vouchers discussed above. SCHIP, established in 1998, now costs $10.2 billion a year in federal spending, and its costs are rising.

Like the modernized AFDC program, Medicaid vouchers should be subject to a work requirement for the able-bodied. Each state could each set the work requirements as it prefers: a minimum number of hours every month to be eligible for a health insurance voucher for the next month, for example. With the federal assistance for Medicaid provided through fixed, finite block grants, each state would bear the marginal costs for weaker or stronger work requirements and be appropriately incentivized to balance costs and benefits.

Work requirements were not prominently considered in scoring the Ryan or Rokita bills. Thus, adoption of work requirements would result in even more savings than CBO projected. States could, and almost certainly would, adopt further cost-saving Medicaid reforms once given the incentives to do so through block grants.

Medicaid block grants would provide each state with incentives to adopt long-overdue reforms to reduce costs for health care and health insurance. States would expand HSAs, adopt tort reform, or eliminate state-mandated benefits in favor of maximum consumer choice over what benefits are covered. Those reduced costs would maximize state gains from the reforms.

Approximately 28 percent of Medicaid spending is for long-term care of the disabled in nursing homes or home health care. This part of the program serves many of the nation's senior citizens. Most of these Medicaid beneficiaries cannot and should not work. They would not necessarily benefit from HSAs or vouchers for the purchase of private health insurance. This is highly expensive care, and under a block-granted program each state would choose how best to address that cost.

The Politics of Medicaid Reform

Support for such fundamental entitlement reform is now mainstream within the Republican Party. As noted above, Ryan included Medicaid block grants in his 2012 and 2013 budgets, both of which were adopted by the Republican-controlled House. A strong majority of the House Republican majority supports extending block grants to Medicaid.

In addition, all of the candidates for the 2012 GOP presidential nomination endorsed the idea of Medicaid block grants, including eventual nominee Mitt Romney. Texas Gov. Rick Perry led 29 Republican governors and the entire Republican Governors Association to endorse the idea as well, garnering support from Govs. Chris Christie (R-NJ), Nikki Haley (R-SC), Bobby Jindal (R-LA), John Kasich (R-OH), Susana Martinez (R-NM), Rick Scott (R-FL), and Scott Walker (R-WI).

The list of block-grant supporters does not include President Barack Obama or any Democrats. Obama falsely called Ryan's Medicaid block grants "the largest cut to Medicaid that has ever been proposed." Would it be accurate to say the 1996 AFDC reforms "cut" that program by 50 percent? Is it rational to oppose reforms that would reduce costs while providing better, higher-quality care through choices, incentives, and competition? Such opposition makes sense only if you are a died-in-the-wool proponent of big government and dependency – and that reveals the fundamental truth about reforms of Medicaid and other entitlements.

The current Medicaid system is so disastrous that those who support it cannot realistically be seen as caring about the poor. Their opposition to reform exposes a radical, impractical, counterproductive ideology to which they are wedded because it maximizes their power.

Notes

1. *Budget of the United States Government, Fiscal Year 2015*, Office of Management and Budget, March 4, 2014, p. 170, Table S-5 Proposed Budget by Category.

2. *Ibid.*

3. National Association of State Budget Officers, "The Fiscal Survey of the States: Spring 2012," page 53, http://www.nasbo.org/publications-data/fiscal-survey-states/fiscal-survey-states-spring-2012, accessed July 2012.

4. Office of the Actuary, Centers for Medicare and Medicaid Services, U.S. Department of Health and Human Services, 2013 Actuarial Report on the Financial Outlook for Medicaid, Washington, DC, p. 24, Table 3.

5. Richard S. Foster, Chief Actuary, Centers for Medicare and Medicaid Services, *Estimated Financial Effects of the Patient Protection and Affordable Care Act, as Amended*, April 22, 2010, p. 6, Table 2; Congressional Budget Office, *The Budget and Economic Outlook: Fiscal Years 2011 to 2021*, January, 2011, p. 62.

6. Scott Gottlieb, "Medicaid Is Worse Than No Coverage at All," *The Wall Street Journal*, March 10, 2011.

7. Joseph Kwok, *et al.*, "The Impact of Health Insurance Status on the Survival of Patients with Head and Neck Cancer," *Cancer* 116, no. 2 (January 2010): pp. 476–485.

8. Michael A. Gaglia Jr., *et al.*, "Effect of Insurance Type on Adverse Cardiac Events After Percutaneous Coronary Intervention," *American Journal of Cardiology* 107, no. 5 (March 2011): pp. 675–80.

9. Damien J. LaPar *et al.*, "Primary Payer Status Affects Mortality For Major Surgical Operations," American Surgical Association 130th Annual Meeting, Chicago, Illinois, April 8–10, 2010.

10. *Ibid.*

11. *Ibid.*

12. Mary Otto, "For Want of a Dentist," *The Washington Post*, February 28, 2007, http://www.washingtonpost.com/wp-dyn/content/article/2007/02/27/AR2007022702116.html.

13. U.S. House of Representatives, Ways and Means Committee, *The 2008 Green Book*, Section 7, Temporary Assistance for Needy Families, Table 7-8, p. 7-27; Gary MacDougal, Kate Campaigne, and Dane Wendell, "Welfare Reform After Ten Years: A State-by-State Analysis," *Report Card*, The Heartland Institute, 2009; Peter Ferrara, *America's Ticking Bankruptcy Bomb* (New York, NY: Harper Collins, 2011), Chapter 5.

14. Ron Haskins, *Work Over Welfare: The Inside Story of the 1996 Welfare Reform Law* (Washington, DC: Brookings Institution, 2006), pp. 336–7; Peter Ferrara, *Ibid.*

15. U.S. House of Representatives, *supra* note 13, Table 7-4, pp. 7-13–7-14; Peter Ferrara, *Ibid.*

16. The Lewin Group, *An Independent Evaluation of Rhode Island's Global Waiver*, December 2011.

17. John C. Goodman and Peter Ferrara, "The Real Reason Health Spending Has Slowed," *Brief Analysis* No. 793, National Center for Policy Analysis, February 12, 2014; Devon Herrick, "A Brief History of Health Savings Accounts," *Brief Analysis* No. 791, National Center for Policy Analysis, December 9, 2013.

6

Repealing and Replacing Obamacare with Patient Power

Much like Social Security, Obamacare can be and must be replaced by free-market reforms that

- expand patient power,[1] giving individuals more control over health care decisions and more choice of providers and treatments;

- ensure health care for all, with no employer mandate and no individual mandate; and

- reduce taxes, federal spending, and regulation.

Unlike Obamacare, such reforms would slow and ultimately reverse the growth of health care costs through proven free-market incentives and competition. Also unlike Obamacare, such reforms would promote job creation, rising wages, economic growth, and general prosperity for working people across America.

Obamacare was sold to the political Left on the prospect of providing universal health insurance coverage. But the Congressional Budget Office (CBO) projects Obamacare will leave 30 million Americans uninsured, even 10 years after its full implementation.[2] Millions of Americans lost their insurance when the individual mandate went into effect, and many millions more will probably lose coverage upon implementation of the employer mandate, originally scheduled to go into effect in 2014 but postponed until 2015 because the Obama administration feared the mandate would hurt

Democrats in the 2014 election.

Obamacare Will Raise Health Care Costs, Not Lower Them

President Barack Obama tried to sell the political Right on Obamacare with the claim it would reduce rapidly rising health care costs. But there was never any foundation for that rhetoric. Expanding third-party coverage of health care spending leaves patients and doctors alike with no incentive to control costs, and that can mean only higher, not lower, costs. The legislation includes various bureaucratic, manipulative schemes touted as controlling costs, but even CBO was not fooled by that. It concluded those bureaucratic measures have no hope of meaningfully reducing health care costs.[3]

Obama repeatedly has tried to take credit for a national trend of slowing health care costs, shown in Figure 1. But that downward cost trend started in 2003, when Obama was a state senator in Illinois, more than 10 years before Obamacare went into effect at the start of 2014.

What happened in 2003? The Republican-majority Congress enacted, and President George W. Bush signed, a measure creating health savings accounts (HSAs). How HSAs created revolutionary market incentives to control health care costs is discussed further below.

The number of HSAs and the amount of money held in them have grown by double digits every year since 2003. In 2012, the number of HSAs grew by 22 percent, with total HSA assets growing by 27 percent to nearly $15.5 billion. HSA assets were projected to grow another 22 percent in 2013, reaching nearly $27 billion.[4]

More than 17 million Americans were estimated to be covered by HSAs at the start of 2014. Nearly 30 million are covered by consumer-directed health plans (CDHPs) of some sort, including HSAs and the health reimbursement accounts (HRAs) more commonly offered by large employers. More Americans today are covered by CDHPs than by patient-unfriendly health maintenance organizations (HMOs).[5]

As Americans embraced CDHPs, national health care spending growth declined, slowing to 3.9 percent each year from 2009 to 2011, and 3.6 percent for 2012,[6] almost two-thirds slower than a decade before. That is the slowest rate of increase since the 1960s, when the federal government's role in health care expanded dramatically.

Obamacare was passed in 2010, as the spending growth decline was underway. With one exception, Obamacare contributed to increasing, not

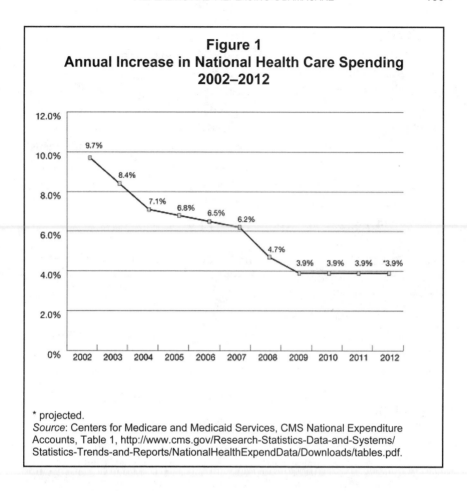

Figure 1
Annual Increase in National Health Care Spending
2002–2012

* projected.
Source: Centers for Medicare and Medicaid Services, CMS National Expenditure Accounts, Table 1, http://www.cms.gov/Research-Statistics-Data-and-Systems/ Statistics-Trends-and-Reports/NationalHealthExpendData/Downloads/tables.pdf.

declining, health care costs. The one exception is the $716 billion in Medicare cuts called for by Obamacare, discussed in Chapter 2.

Except for the Medicare cuts, which do not involve any actual health care reform, Obamacare is likely to increase health care costs. In their September 3, 2014 report on national health care expenditures,[7] Department of Health and Human Services actuaries projected the rate of annual health care spending increases would grow from 3.6 percent in 2013 to 5.6 percent in 2014 (when Obamacare went into effect), and then continue at 6 percent a year on average through the rest of the decade. That means health care spending as a share of GDP grew from 16.2 percent in 2007 to 17.2 percent in 2013 and is projected to reach 19.3 percent in 2023. As *The Wall Street Journal* noted in an unsigned editorial, "In other words, health care will soak up nearly one of every five U.S. dollars, instead of one in six."[8]

The actuaries attributed the accelerating growth in health care spending at least in part to "spending growth associated with the coverage expansions in the Affordable Care Act (ACA) in 2014 and beyond," such as the 23 percent expansion in Medicaid enrollment resulting from Obamacare. Notably, they attributed the pre-Obamacare slowdown in health care spending growth in part to "increases in cost-sharing for people with private health insurance" and "additional increases in cost-sharing requirements, including continuing increases in the adoption of high deductible plans,"[9] meaning CDHPs. They noted even rapid cost increases under Obamacare "would be dampened somewhat by ... the ongoing trend toward higher cost-sharing requirements for the privately insured."[10]

Obamacare Reduces Jobs, Incomes, and Economic Growth

One of the biggest drags on economic growth under President Barack Obama will be Obamacare. That drag will come primarily from the sweeping overregulation it imposes.

The biggest culprit is the employer mandate, which requires all employers of 50 or more full-time employees to buy their employees health insurance with terms and benefits specified by the federal government. That is effectively a tax on employment, more than $10,000 a year per employee with family coverage.

Even for employers that already provide health insurance, the mandate is likely to represent a big tax increase, because the mandated health insurance will likely cost more than what the employer is already providing. As they are wont to do, politicians and bureaucrats responded to political pressure to include in the mandated health insurance generous benefits most people will think the employer is paying for. That will drive up the cost of the insurance.

Moreover, the mandated health insurance is subject to costly guaranteed issue and community rating requirements. Guaranteed issue requires insurers to sell health insurance to everyone who applies, regardless of how sick they are when they first apply. That is like requiring homeowners insurance companies to sell fire insurance to buyers who apply after their house has caught fire.

Community rating requires health insurers to sell health insurance to everyone at the same standard premium rates, without regard to how sick (and therefore costly) an applicant may be when he or she first applies. That is like requiring homeowners insurance companies to sell fire insurance to an applicant whose house has already caught fire for the *same premium* charged to those whose houses have not burned down.

Of course, if homeowners insurance companies were subjected to guaranteed issue and community rating requirements, the standard premiums would be very high. The same is true for health insurance. There are better, less costly ways of ensuring health insurance is available to everyone.

To avoid the costly tax on employment resulting from the employer mandate, millions of employees across the country have been reduced to a part-time work schedule of 29 hours a week or less, because the Obamacare definition of a full-time employee is 30 hours a week or more. That is driving down the net wages of middle-income and working-poor Americans and increasing economic inequality as a result. Small companies currently near the employer mandate's 50-employee threshold are reconsidering any plans they might have had to add employees.

Clearly, the employer mandate has been slowing economic growth, stunting the recovery, and extending the misery of the recession well beyond the record of previous recessions. Similarly, the individual mandate – which requires most Americans to obtain health insurance or pay a tax penalty – is increasing the costs of health insurance in the individual market and having a similar negative impact on the economy.

The employer mandate and the individual mandate are effectively tax increases, which are a drag on economic growth. Obamacare is financed directly by another half-trillion dollars in tax increases, which are also anti-growth.

Three Reforms, Health Care for All ...

Outlined below is a plan for repealing and replacing Obamacare with free-market, patient-centered health care reforms. Just three reforms will achieve health care for all – and, as shown in the next section, lower health care costs as well.

Universal Health Insurance Tax Credit

The centerpiece of patient power is extending to everyone the tax preference enjoyed today only by those who receive employer-provided health insurance. This should take the form of a refundable universal health insurance tax credit of roughly $2,500 per person per year ($8,000 for a family of four) for the purchase of private health insurance, as proposed by longtime patient power advocate John C. Goodman.[11] That $2,500 would not be meant to pay for the entire cost of such insurance, only to help pay for it, just as the tax preference for employer-provided insurance does not pay the entire cost of such insurance.

The credit would provide an incentive to purchase health insurance. By capping the credit, the plan ensures there is no incentive to buy unnecessarily expensive health insurance, as would be true of an open-ended deduction for health insurance. Moreover, the capped credit would provide everyone with an equal tax benefit for purchasing health insurance, rather than the widely varying and arbitrary tax benefits under Obamacare.

The insurance purchased by an individual with the tax credit would belong to the individual, not to his or her employer, and so it would be fully portable, following the employee to any job he or she may choose. Employees would be free to use the tax credit to purchase a health insurance plan other than the one provided by their employers, including health savings accounts (HSAs).

Once a health insurance plan is purchased, renewability would be guaranteed as long as the premiums continued to be paid. No one's premium could be increased higher than the premium for others in the same initial risk class. Such guaranteed renewability is required by current law – indeed going back to the common law – because guaranteed renewability protecting against the costs of getting sick is what health insurance contracts promise. That requirement became federal law in the Health Insurance Portability and Accountability Act (HIPAA) of 1996.

A person who chooses not to purchase health insurance would not receive the credit. But there would be no penalty for failing to comply with any mandate, because there is no mandate of any sort in the patient power alternative to Obamacare. For every person in every household that files a tax return without claiming the credit, the $2,500 would fund care for the poor and uninsured in the taxpayer's community – an automatic funding mechanism for a health care safety net.

No government mandate would require the credit be used to buy any particular insurance with any particular terms or benefits. Each individual, including employees who have employer-provided coverage but would prefer to choose insurance of their own, would be free to use the credit to buy the health insurance of his or her choice. That provides working people with an important check on the insurance the employer may choose for the company's employees, which may be designed more to suit the employer's interests than the employees'.

Employees would even be free to use the credit to buy into coverage through Medicaid. The credit amount is roughly equal to the CBO-estimated average cost of adding one person to Medicaid coverage. This feature would ensure coverage for anyone with a preexisting condition, because Medicaid is required to cover everyone regardless of preexisting conditions. Few people, of course, would choose Medicaid, for reasons discussed below. More likely, current Medicaid beneficiaries would use the credit to leave that program and purchase private health insurance.

Some observers worry the universal health insurance tax credit would cause employers to drop their current coverage, a problem that currently afflicts Obamacare. But there's no reason for that to happen under a patient power replacement. Employers who provide health insurance for their employees will continue to deduct that expense from their taxes as a cost of doing business, just as they do their employees' wages. For employees, there would be no net tax increase, as the tax credit would simply replace the current tax exclusion they receive for the value of employer-provided insurance.

Block-Granting Medicaid to the States

The second component of patient power reforms would be to transfer control over Medicaid to the states, as discussed in Chapter 4. Federal financing would be provided through fixed, finite, block grants to each state, as under the successful 1996 reforms of the Aid to Families with Dependent Children (AFDC) welfare program. Currently, federal financing for Medicaid is provided under a matching formula that pays more to each state the more it spends on Medicaid.

With a fixed, finite, block grant, state officials know if they redesign their Medicaid program to cost more, their taxpayers will pay 100 percent of the difference. If their redesigned program costs less, 100 percent of the savings remains with the state. These are ideal incentives for each state to weigh the costs against the benefits for Medicaid spending.

Preferably, each state would use its power under the Medicaid block grants to provide assistance to the poor through health insurance vouchers the beneficiaries could use to supplement the universal health insurance tax credit to help them obtain private health insurance. Each state would determine how much assistance at what income levels would be necessary to ensure the state's poor could buy essential health insurance. Those levels would be very different for Louisiana and Mississippi than for California and New York, given their widely varying health care cost structures and income levels.

With private health insurance made affordable by the universal health insurance tax credit, supplemented for the poor with Medicaid health insurance vouchers, low-income families could enjoy the same health care as their middle-income neighbors, because they would have the same health insurance. Competitive market pressures, moreover, would force the insurance companies to pay enough to doctors and hospitals to ensure those covered by the insurance can get timely, essential health care. The patient power reforms described here would consequently represent an enormous benefit for the poor as compared to the current Medicaid program.

CBO has scored the Medicaid block grant proposal as saving nearly $1 trillion over the first 10 years alone.

Risk Pools for the Uninsurable

States would be free to use part of the Medicaid block grants to set up risk pools to provide coverage to those uninsured who are too sick, and therefore too costly, to obtain insurance in the market. Those insured by the pools would pay premiums based on their ability to pay, so the pools would serve a safety net function.

Thirty states had established such risk pools before Obamacare. They proved to be a low-cost means of providing for the treatment of preexisting conditions for those who were uninsured when they contracted a very costly illness, such as cancer or heart disease. Such pools are low-cost because only relatively small numbers of people become truly uninsurable in the private market. Risk pools are less expensive and less distorting of the insurance market than guaranteed issue and community rating regulations, which raise health insurance costs sharply for everyone, creating more uninsured as a result.

Health Care for All

Unlike Obamacare, the three reforms outlined above – tax credits, Medicaid block grants, and risk pools – would ensure universal health care for all. Everyone would receive the universal health insurance tax credit, which they could use to help pay for the health insurance of their choice. Once insured, current law guarantees renewability of that coverage as long as they continue to pay the premiums, and those premiums could not be raised higher for someone who became ill than for others in the same initial risk class. The poor would get additional assistance through the Medicaid vouchers, empowering them to get essential health coverage. The uninsured who had become uninsurable could turn to the risk pool for their coverage or use their tax credit to buy into Medicaid.

... and Lower Health Care Costs, as Well
The patient power reforms described above make health insurance coverage available to all, and they reduce the growth in health care costs at the same time.

Health Savings Accounts
Health savings accounts (HSAs) would be included among the insurance options available to all through patient power reforms. They pair savings accounts for small or routine expenses with high-deductible health insurance for catastrophic or unexpected expenses.

The insurance component, with a deductible in the range of $2,000 to $6,000 a year, pays for health expenses over the deductible. Such high-deductible insurance costs substantially less than more traditional, first-dollar-coverage insurance. The premium savings would be deposited in the savings account and used to pay for health care expenses below the deductible. Any funds that remain in the savings account at year-end roll over to the next year, accumulating to pay for future health care expenses or to spend on anything in retirement.

HSAs reduce the growth in health care costs by giving patients incentives to become cost-conscious consumers of health care: The more careful they are with their spending, the more funds will accumulate in their savings accounts. HSAs also give doctors and hospitals incentives to lower their prices in order to attract those newly cost-conscious consumers. The cost-cutting incentives flow all the way through to the developers of health care technology, who are spurred by market incentives to develop technology that reduces health care costs in addition to improving health care quality and effectiveness.

After one healthy year, the typical consumer with an HSA will have more than enough in the savings account to pay for all expenses below the insurance component's deductible. Moreover, patients with HSAs enjoy complete control over how to spend their savings account funds. They don't need the approval of their insurance company to spend their funds on whatever health care they want.

HSAs can be especially beneficial for vulnerable populations, particularly the sick and the poor. Because they have complete control over their savings account funds, those who need health care become empowered consumers in the medical marketplace. Because they can pay for care themselves out of their savings accounts, the poor have ready access to a wide range of providers, unlike under Medicaid today, and they can use the funds to pay for effective preventive care, a missing component of care for many of the poor.[12]

HSAs and the incentives they provide have proven very effective in controlling costs in the real world. A 2012 RAND Corporation study found persons covered by HSAs on average spend 21 percent less on health care in the first year after switching from more traditional coverage. RAND estimated national health care costs would fall by nearly $60 billion if half of all employees were covered by HSAs.[13] Annual cost increases for HSAs have run 50 percent less than for conventional health care coverage, and in some years HSA premiums have not increased at all.[14]

Controlling Health Care Costs

The market-based HSA incentives become more effective at controlling health care costs the more people are covered by HSAs. Through the patient power reforms, HSAs would become available to everyone in the health care marketplace. Medicaid beneficiaries would enjoy the freedom to choose HSAs for their Medicaid coverage. Employees would enjoy the freedom to choose HSAs through the universal insurance tax credit if their employers did not offer them. Senior citizens on Medicare would enjoy the freedom to choose HSAs through Medicare Part C.

Choice, market incentives, and competition among insurers to attract consumers newly empowered with the universal health care tax credit would further reduce health care costs. Allowing the sale of insurance across state lines and implementing medical malpractice reform would complete a highly effective reform package to control health care costs.

The patient power approach is the polar opposite of Obamacare, which largely increases health care costs through the distorted incentives and expense of extended, overregulated, third-party payment health insurance coverage.

Restoring Economic Growth, Jobs, and Prosperity

Repealing Obamacare and replacing it with patient power would junk the federal overregulation of health care and insurance imposed by Obama's ill-conceived program. Gone would be the employer mandate and the individual mandate, two onerous taxes on employment. They would be replaced by freedom of choice and competition, with each consumer free to choose the health insurance he or she wants in a competitive marketplace.

Patient power would mean the end of the Obama-era 29-hour work week. The Bureau of Labor Statistics (BLS) reports more than seven million Americans are currently stuck in involuntary part-time employment. "These individuals were working part-time because their hours had been cut back or because they were unable to find a full-time job," BLS reports.[15] Repealing the employer mandate's effective tax on employment would increase employment and jobs. The return of the 40-hour work week would lead to the return of rising wages and incomes for middle-income and working people. That increased labor input to the economy, in turn, would increase economic growth and prosperity.

Patient power also would remove regulations imposing guaranteed issue and community rating, resulting in a sharp reduction in health insurance costs. Further reductions would result from the broad availability of health savings accounts throughout the nation's health care marketplace. Competition and market incentives created by the capped universal health insurance tax credit would further reduce costs, as would the liberation of national competition as insurance is allowed to be bought and sold across state borders. Medical malpractice reform would further reduce costs.

All told, the lower health care costs achieved by patient power reforms would effectively constitute a major tax cut for the economy, increasing economic growth and prosperity. The repeal of Obamacare also would reverse trillions of dollars in direct tax increases under the act. That would mean a 16 percent reduction in the capital gains tax and the tax on corporate dividends, and nearly a 25 percent reduction in the Medicare payroll tax.

Reversing tax increases on capital gains and corporate dividends promotes capital investment, the economic foundation for increased jobs and higher wages. Other tax increases under Obamacare, such as the medical device tax and the tax on health insurance, directly raise the cost of health care and insurance. Repealing them would constitute another tax cut.

Conclusion

Repealing and replacing Obamacare with patient power would ensure health care for all, which Obamacare dismally fails to do. Patient power also would deliver on the promise of reducing health care costs; Obamacare does the opposite. Patient power would reverse the Obamacare drag on the economy, restoring economic growth, jobs, and prosperity.

Patient power would accomplish all of this while repealing the employer mandate, the individual mandate, and other costly regulations, replacing them with freedom of choice and control over health care, market incentives, and market competition. It would constitute a pro-growth tax cut of trillions of dollars over the years and reduce federal spending by trillions of dollars as well.

Too many self-appointed wise men in Washington are saying we can no longer repeal Obamacare because doing so would cause millions of people to lose their Obamacare insurance and benefits. That fear-mongering rings hollow in light of the positive, populist, pro-growth, win-win entitlement reforms proposed in this book – reforms that can fundamentally transform not only health care but also Social Security, Medicare, Medicaid, and welfare.

Obamacare is based on central planning, coercive mandates prescribing from the top down exactly what health insurance everyone must buy. Such central planning naturally involves banning many existing health insurance policies people previously had, liked, and were promised they could keep. The patient power replacement for Obamacare is based on unrestricted individual consumer choice in a competitive marketplace.

Voters will wildly and widely applaud replacing Obamacare with patient power.

Notes

1. John C. Goodman and Gerald L. Musgrave, *Patient Power: The Free-Enterprise Alternative to Clinton's Health Plan* (Washington, DC: Cato Institute, October 1992). See also John C. Goodman, *Priceless: Curing the Healthcare Crisis* (Oakland, CA: The Independent Institute, June 2012).

2. Douglas Elmendorf, Congressional Budget Office, Letter to the Honorable Nancy Pelosi, March 20, 2010.

3. Letter from CBO Director Douglas Elmendorf to the Honorable Senator Harry Reid, Cost Estimate, H.R. 3950, Patient Protection and Affordable Care Act, March 11, 2010; Congressional Budget Office, *The Long Term Budget Outlook, July 2014*; Office of the Actuary, Centers for Medicare and Medicaid Services, National Health Expenditures, 2013 to 2023, September 17, 2014.

4. America's Health Insurance Plans (AHIP), "January 2014 Census Shows 17.4 Million Enrollees in Health Savings Account-Eligible High Deductible Plans (HSA/HDHPs)," May 2014; John C. Goodman and Peter Ferrara, "The Real Reason Health Spending Has Slowed," NCPA *Brief Analysis* No. 793, February 13, 2014; Peter Ferrara, "Obamacare Is the Problem, Health Savings Accounts Are the Solution," NCPA *Issue Brief* No. 124, July 2013.

5. America's Health Insurance Plans, *ibid.*; John C. Goodman and Peter Ferrara, *ibid.*; Peter Ferrara, *ibid.*; Greg Scandlen, "Ten Ways Consumer Driven Health Care Is a Proven Success," *Policy Study* No. 125, The Heartland Institute, January 2010.

6. Figure 1 shows 3.9 percent, but that was an estimate at the time the CMS report was written. The final figure for 2012, as reported by CMS, was 3.6 percent.

7. Andrea M. Sisko, *et al.*, "National Health Expenditure Projections, 2013–2023: Faster Growth Expected with Expanded Coverage and Improving Economy," *Health Affairs*, Vol. 33, no. 10 (2014), http://content.healthaffairs.org/content/33/10/1841

8. "The ObamaCare Escalator," *The Wall Street Journal,* September 6–7, 2014, p. A14, http://online.wsj.com/articles/the-obamacare-escalator-1409957215.

9. Andrea M. Sisko, *et al.*, *supra* note 7, p. 1.

10. *Ibid.*

11. John C. Goodman and Gerald L. Musgrave, *supra* note 1.

12. Center for Poverty Research, University of California Davis, "How Is Poverty Related to Access to Care and Preventive Healthcare," http://poverty.ucdavis.edu/faq/how-poverty-related-access-care-and-preventive-healthcare.

13. John C. Goodman and Peter Ferrara, *supra* note 4.

14. *Ibid.*

15. Bureau of Labor Statistics, *Employment Situation Summary*, September 5, 2014.

7

The Foundation for Reform: Get America Booming Again

The U.S. economy sustained a real rate of annual economic growth of 3.3 percent from 1945 to 1973, and it achieved the same 3.3 percent sustained real growth from 1982 to 2007.[1] It was only during the stagflation decade of 1973–1982, reflecting the deeply misguided reigning intellectual leadership of the time, that real growth fell to only half the long-term trend. As explained by Brian Domitrovic in his book *Econoclasts*, "The unique ability of the United States to maintain a historic rate of economic growth over the long term is what has rendered this nation the world's lone 'hyperpower.'"[2]

President Barack Obama returned to the proven-failed economic policies of the 1970s, and as should be expected, he got quite similar results. If we could revive and sustain America's historic 3.3 percent real growth for 20 years, our total economic production (GDP) would double in that time. After 30 years, our economic output would grow by two and two-thirds. After 40 years, our prosperity bounty would grow by three and two-thirds.

The restoration of America's long-term economic growth trend is the foundation for successful entitlement reform. Such booming but attainable growth would maximize available revenues to cover the nation's entitlement liabilities. With a booming economy, more jobs with higher wages reduce the number of people dependent on welfare. More people would be able to afford health care coverage or get it from their employers. And retirement savings and investment would earn robust returns.

We know how to recreate the world-leading American prosperity of the past. The principles of economic growth are timeless and have worked everywhere they have been tried, throughout human history. We can look back to what we did to get out of trouble the last time the U.S. economy ran off the rails, in the disastrous 1970s. What we did then to restore booming economic growth and rescue the American Dream is instructive for what we need to do now.

A big problem today is that no one under 40 is old enough to have experienced the 1970s, and most of those over 40 have so enjoyed the prosperity of the nearly 30 years until 2008 that they have forgotten those bad old days.

Keynesians Slow the U.S. Economy in the 1970s

The economics of the 1970s really begins in 1969. Inflation had climbed to 5.5 percent that year, up from 1.6 percent in 1965. To counter that, the Federal Reserve slammed on the monetary brakes. That resulted in a recession beginning in December 1969, ending the 1960s economic boom that had stemmed from the sweeping income tax rate cuts under President John F. Kennedy. The Fed returned to easy money to get the economy growing again, and the recession ended in 11 months.

But with the easy money to end the recession, by 1973 inflation reached 6.2 percent, even higher than before. So the Fed reversed itself again to tight money to counter the inflation. That produced the steepest recession of the postwar era at the time, starting in November 1973 and lasting 16 months. Somehow, inflation also reached a new peak of 11 percent in 1974, followed by 9.1 percent in 1975. Under the reigning economic doctrine of the time, Keynesian economics, this mix of simultaneous inflation and recession was not possible. Physics says the bumblebee should not be able to fly, still the bee does fly.

Keynesian economics arose in the 1930s in response to the Great Depression. The doctrine holds economic growth is stimulated by increased government spending, deficits, and debt. That is supposed to increase aggregate demand, which is supposed to lead to increased production to satisfy that demand, thus restoring economic growth. It didn't work in the 1930s, as the recession of 1929 extended into the decade-long Great Depression.[3] It didn't work because the money for the increased government spending has to come from somewhere in the private sector, either through taxes or borrowing (or possibly inflation), resulting in no net increase in demand at all. And more fundamentally, the foundation for booming economic growth is not increasing demand, which is insatiable, and so can never be inadequate, but increasing production or output (supply). In other words, just as an individual cannot spend himself rich, neither can a nation.

Keynesian economics argues recessions are caused by too little aggregate demand and inflation is caused by too much aggregate demand. Since it is impossible to have both too much and too little demand at the same time, a combination of recession and inflation is not supposed to be possible under this doctrine. Yet somehow the United States suffered 8.5 percent unemployment in 1975, up from 3.5 percent in 1969, to go with the 9.1 percent inflation in 1975. That led many people to begin to doubt the reigning Keynesian orthodoxy.

The Fed returned to easy money to end the steep 1973–75 recession, and by 1979 inflation was back to a new peak of 11.3 percent. In 1980, inflation roared to 13.5 percent even as the economy suffered still another recession, this one lasting six months. Prices had risen 25 percent in just two years.

Soaring inflation also caused interest rates to rise, as lenders will not otherwise lend their money during a time of rapid inflation, only to be paid back in dollars worth so much less than the dollars they lent. The prime interest rate reached 21.5 percent in 1980,[4] with home mortgage interest rates soon climbing as high as 14.7 percent.[5] With the downdrafts of inflation and sky-high interest rates, unemployment began an upward climb during the years under President Jimmy Carter, eventually peaking at more than 10 percent in 1982.[6]

The poverty rate started rising in 1978, eventually climbing by 33 percent, from 11.4 percent to 15.2 percent.[7] A fall in real median family income that began in 1978 snowballed to a decline of almost 10 percent by 1982.[8] Average real family income for the lowest-income 20 percent declined by 14.2 percent.[9] During the Carter years (1977 to 1980), real income declined for every income quintile, from the lowest 20 percent to the highest 20 percent.[10] Real average income of U.S. households was, in fact, in a long-term decline from 1970 to 1980.[11] In addition, from 1968 to 1982, the Dow Jones Industrial Average lost 70 percent of its real value, reflecting the overall collapse of stocks.[12] This all reflected roaring inflation, engineered by Keynesian monetary policies of the 1970s, which was depreciating the real incomes of working people.

In the 1964 James Bond movie classic *Goldfinger*, archvillain Auric

Goldfinger plots a dirty-bomb attack on the U.S. gold reserves at Fort Knox that would leave the reserves poisoned by deadly radiation for more than 50 years. While the plot is underway, Goldfinger, aided by a Red Chinese agent seeking economic chaos in the West, gloats to his prisoner, Bond, that he conservatively estimates the value of his own gold stock will soar by ten times as a result. The plot is foiled only because Bond is able to seduce Goldfinger's lover, provocatively named Pussy Galore in the movie, into helping him. As a result of Galore's double-cross of Goldfinger, Bond is able to defuse the bomb with 0:07 seconds left on the timer.

Proving truth is stranger than fiction, in the 1970s U.S. economic policies were able to more than achieve the results sought by Goldfinger and his Red Chinese agent through their evil plot, as Domitrovic explains in *Econoclasts*.[13] In 1964 the price of gold was fixed at $35 per ounce. By 1979, it had soared to ten times that, to $350 an ounce. By just the next year, 1980, the price had more than doubled again, to $800.

Reaganomics to the Rescue

Reagan explicitly scrapped Keynesian economics in favor of the new supply-side economics, which holds that economic growth results from incentives for increased production, rather than from supposedly increased demand caused by greater government spending, deficits, and debt. Reagan assigned to the Fed and monetary policy the sole goal of reducing inflation through tight-money policies. To stimulate the economy, Reagan adopted supply-side policies to sharply increase incentives through lower tax rates and reduced regulatory burdens.

Reagan had campaigned on a recovery plan with four specific components, which he then implemented after he was elected:

- cuts in tax rates to restore incentives for economic growth, implemented first with a reduction in the top income tax rate of 70 percent down to 50 percent, and then a 25 percent across-the-board reduction in income tax rates for everyone. The 1986 tax reform reduced tax rates further, leaving just two rates, 28 percent and 15 percent. Federal tax revenue doubled in the 1980s, reflecting the restoration of booming economic growth.

- spending reductions, including a $31 billion cut in spending in 1981, close to 5 percent of the federal budget then, or the equivalent of about

$175 billion in spending cuts for the year today. In constant dollars, nondefense discretionary spending declined by 14.4 percent from 1981 to 1982, and by 16.8 percent from 1981 to 1983.[14] Moreover, in constant dollars this nondefense discretionary spending never returned to its 1981 level for the rest of Reagan's two terms.[15] By 1988, spending was still down 14.4 percent from its 1981 level in constant dollars.[16] Even with the Reagan defense buildup, which famously won the Cold War without firing a shot, total federal spending declined from a high of 23.5 percent of GDP in 1983 to 21.3 percent in 1988 and 21.2 percent in 1989.[17] That's a real reduction in the size of government relative to the economy of 10 percent.

- anti-inflation monetary policy restraining money supply growth compared to demand, to maintain a stable value of the dollar.

- deregulation, which saved consumers an estimated $100 billion per year in lower prices. Reagan's first executive order eliminated price controls on oil and natural gas. Production soared, and the price of oil declined by more than 50 percent.

These policies worked spectacularly, amounting to the most successful economic experiment in world history. The Reagan recovery started in official records in November 1982 and lasted 92 months without a recession until July 1990, when the tax increases of the 1990 budget deal under President George H.W. Bush killed it.[18] That set a new record for the longest peacetime expansion ever, the previous peacetime high having been 58 months.[19]

During this seven-year recovery, the economy grew by almost one-third, the equivalent of adding the entire economy of West Germany, the third-largest economy in the world at the time, to the U.S. economy.[20] In 1984 alone, real economic growth boomed by 6.8 percent, the highest in 50 years.[21] Nearly 20 million new jobs were created during this recovery, increasing U.S. civilian employment by almost 20 percent.[22] Unemployment fell to 5.3 percent by 1989.[23]

Real per-capita disposable income increased by 18 percent from 1982 to 1989, meaning the U.S. standard of living increased by almost 20 percent, reversing the Carter declines.[24] The Carter decline in income for the bottom 20 percent of individuals was reversed as well, with average real household income for this group rising by 12.2 percent from 1983 to 1989.[25] The poverty rate, which had started increasing during the Carter years, declined every year from 1984 to 1989, dropping by one-sixth from its peak.[26]

The rise in inflation during the Carter years was likewise spectacularly reversed. Inflation was reduced by more than half between 1980 and 1982, to 6.2 percent.[27] It was cut in half again in 1983, to 3.2 percent.[28] The contractionary tight-money policies that killed this inflation inexorably created the steep recession of 1981 to 1982, which is why Reagan did not suffer politically catastrophic blame for that recession.

By 1987 the prime rate was cut by two-thirds, to 8.2 percent, on its way down to 6.25 percent by 1992.[29] New home mortgage interest rates also declined steadily, reaching 9.2 percent in 1988, on their way down to 8 percent by 1992.[30] Opponents of the Reagan tax cuts had argued they would increase interest rates.

The stock market more than tripled in value between 1980 and 1990, a larger increase than in any previous decade.[31] Real personal assets rose by nearly $6 trillion, from $15.5 trillion in 1980 to $21.1 trillion in 1990, an increase of 36 percent.[32] Total real private net worth rose by $4.3 trillion between 1980 and 1989, totaling $17.1 trillion in constant dollars, an increase of one-third.[33]

In their 2008 book, *The End of Prosperity*, supply side guru Art Laffer, then *Wall Street Journal* chief financial writer Steve Moore, and Peter J. Tanous point out this Reagan recovery grew into a 25-year boom, with only slight interruptions by shallow, short recessions in 1990 and 2001. They write:

> We call this period, 1982–2007, the twenty-five year boom – the greatest period of wealth creation in the history of the planet. In 1980, the net worth – assets minus liabilities – of all U.S. households and business ... was $25 trillion in today's dollars. By 2007, ... net worth was just shy of $57 trillion. Adjusting for inflation, more wealth was created in America in the twenty-five year boom than in the previous two hundred years.[34]

They add, "The economy in real terms is almost twice as large today as it was in the late 1970s."[35]

Similarly, Steve Forbes wrote in *Forbes* magazine in 2008,

Between the early 1980s and 2007 we lived in an economic Golden Age. Never before have so many people advanced so far economically in so short a period of time as they have during the last 25 years. Until the credit crisis, 70 million people a year [worldwide] were joining the middle class. The U.S. kicked off this long boom with the economic reforms of Ronald Reagan, particularly his enormous income tax cuts. We burst from the economic stagnation of the 1970s into a dynamic, innovative, high tech-oriented economy. Even in recent years the much maligned U.S. did well. Between year-end 2002 and year-end 2007 U.S. growth exceeded the entire size of China's economy.[36]

In other words, the *growth* in the U.S. economy from 2002 to 2007 was the equivalent of adding the entire economy of China to that of the United States.

Gingrich, Clinton, and Bush Extend the Boom

Contributing to this extension of the Reagan recovery into the 25-year boom were the tax cuts and other pro-growth policies adopted by the Gingrich-led congressional majorities in the 1990s, and the much-maligned Bush tax cuts adopted in 2001 and 2003. Congressional Republicans pushed through a capital gains tax rate cut of nearly 30 percent in 1997, from 28 percent down to 20 percent, expanded IRAs, and implemented other tax cuts on capital. Despite the 30 percent capital gains rate cut, actual capital gains revenues were $84 billion higher for 1997–2000 than projected before the rate cut.[37]

Gingrich's Republicans also cut spending, though Republicans later lost control of spending after Gingrich left in 1998. Total federal discretionary spending, as well as the subcategory of nondefense discretionary spending, declined from 1995 to 1996 in actual nominal dollars. In constant dollars, adjusted for inflation, the decline was 5.4 percent. By 2000, total federal discretionary spending was still about the same as in 1995 in constant dollars. As a percent of GDP, federal discretionary spending was slashed by 17.5 percent in just four years, from 1995 to 1999. Total federal spending relative to GDP declined from 1995 to 2000 by 12.5 percent, a reduction in the federal government relative to the economy of about one-eighth, in just five years.

This was accomplished not just by reducing discretionary spending but also through fundamental structural reforms of some programs. The old Aid to Families with Dependent Children (AFDC) program, for example, was replaced with a new system that sent funding to the states in fixed, finite block grants that sharply reduced poverty while cutting federal spending on the program by 50 percent compared to where it would have been based on prior trends. In addition, Depression-era farm subsidy programs were phased out under the Freedom to Farm reforms. Unfortunately, this subsidy phase-out was later reversed under President George W. Bush and House Speaker Dennis Hastert.

Note this spending reduction in the face of the economic boom contradicted both Keynesian economics and the central pillar of Obamanomics, that government spending is what drives economic growth. Gingrich and Clinton cut spending, and the economy boomed and boomed.

In 2001, Bush again cut tax rates for everyone, as Reagan had. But Bush cut the lower-income rates by a bigger percentage than the higher-income rates. He reduced the top marginal income tax rate from 39.6 percent to 35 percent, a reduction of 11 percent, while he cut the rate for the lowest-income individuals by 33 percent, from 15 percent to 10 percent. In 2003, Bush cut the capital gains tax rate by 25 percent and the income tax rate on corporate dividends by more than half.

Though Obama insisted on calling these Bush tax cuts the "failed economic policies of the past," they quickly ended the 2001 recession despite the contractionary economic impacts of 9/11. The economy continued to grow for another 73 months. After the rate cuts were fully implemented in 2003, the economy created 7.8 million new jobs and the unemployment rate fell from more than 6 percent to 4.4 percent.[38] Real economic growth over the next three years doubled from the average for the prior three years, to 3.5 percent.[39]

In response to the rate cuts, business investment spending, which had declined for nine straight quarters, reversed and increased by 6.7 percent per quarter.[40] That is where the jobs came from. Manufacturing output soared to its highest level in 20 years.[41] The stock market revived, creating almost $7 trillion in new shareholder wealth.[42] From 2003 to 2007, the S&P 500 almost doubled. Capital gains tax revenues had doubled by 2005 in the wake of the 25 percent rate cut.[43]

The deficit in the last budget adopted by Republican congressional majorities was $161 billion for fiscal 2007. The day the Democrat congressional majorities took office, January 3, 2007, the unemployment rate was 4.6 percent. Bush's economic policies, "the failed policies of the past" according to Obama's rhetoric, had set a record of 52 straight months of job creation.

By 2007, the 25-year economic boom had created 50 million new jobs and restored the long-term U.S. economic growth rate to more than 3 percent per year. As Professor Henry R. Nau explained in *The Wall Street Journal* on January 26, 2012,

> the U.S. grew by more than 3 percent per year [in real terms] from 1980 to 2007, and created more than 50 million new jobs, massively expanding a middle class of working women, African-Americans and legal as well as illegal immigrants. Per capita income increased by 65 percent, and household income went up substantially in all income categories.[44]

Nau added,

> Yes, "the middle class has shrunk," as Mr. Obama said while campaigning last month. But not because it's getting poorer, but because it's getting richer. According to Stephen Rose of the Georgetown University Center on Education and the Workforce, fewer people live today in middle-class households with incomes between $35,000 and $105,000, while the percentage of households making less than $35,000 has remained the same. Where did the missing households go? They became richer. In the past three decades [1980 to 2007], the percentage of households making more than $105,000 in inflation adjusted dollars doubled to 24 percent from 11 percent.[45]

So Reagan's policies transformed double-digit inflation, double-digit unemployment, double-digit interest rates with subpar growth about half the long-term U.S. average, declining real wages and incomes, and soaring poverty into a 25-year boom restoring the long-term U.S. growth trend line, and ultimately full employment, while slaying a historic inflation that remains tamed to this day and achieving rising real wages and incomes and consistently declining poverty. During this Long Boom, as economists have called it, more wealth was created than during any prior comparable period in world history, and the U.S. boom actually began to spread worldwide, starting to lift Third World populations into middle-income living standards. The turnaround and these results are what make it the greatest economic boom in world history, and a heroic achievement deserving of much greater recognition and reward for the major policymakers who led its creation.

Superficial critics focus on the federal budget deficits during the Reagan years. But the largest Reagan deficit was $225 billion, a small fraction of Obama's multiple, record-shattering deficits of well over a trillion dollars a year for four years, when no prior deficit in history was ever anywhere near a trillion dollars. This is true regardless of whether the relative deficits are measured in real or in constant dollars, or as a percent of GDP.

But the most important point is that the deficits and debt of the Reagan years were quite manageable given the economic growth of the time, because they did not affect any real-world economic factors, such as unemployment, inflation, economic growth, income growth, poverty, interest rates, etc., all of which turned around during those years from very negative trends to very positive ones. That is why the Reagan deficit criticism is much ado about nothing. If the deficits and debt had caused inflation, rising unemployment, declining wages and incomes, and more poverty, that would have been a serious problem. But just the opposite happened during the Reagan years and beyond, which is why it is false to brand the deficits a serious problem.

Reagan faced three main challenges when he came into office: the flagging economy, weakening national defense, and the budget deficit and its contribution to the national debt. Economic and political constraints meant he could solve only two of those three. He picked the right ones, getting the economy booming, which reduced the effective deficit as a percent of GDP, and winning the Cold War without firing a shot. By the time Reagan left office in 1989, the federal deficit was down to 2.8 percent of GDP, and although the national debt as a percent of GDP did rise during those years, it was still far below its peak at the end of World War II – a peak Obama is now taking us back to in peacetime. Also when Reagan left office in 1989, the Soviet Union was in terminal collapse.

The Reagan deficits were not major economy-threatening problems, and their effects did not show up in any real-world economic indicators. Yet, the same Washington establishment that complained about his deficits so bitterly then told us the Obama deficits were pro-growth, under their

Keynesian witchcraft doctrines. But Obama's deficits drained the economy and racked up record-breaking deficits and debt because they were not tied to income tax rate cuts and pro-growth regulatory reform.

The Financial Crisis: How the Government Caused It

The 25-year Reagan economic boom ended in 2008 with the bursting of the housing bubble and the resulting financial crisis. That was caused not by the market, or "Wall Street bankers," or tax cuts and deregulation, but by the government, through policies departing from every one of the four planks of Reaganomics.

A central theme of Obama's 2012 reelection campaign was that we can't go back to the same economic policies that caused "the mess we are in," by which he meant the 2008 financial crisis. Obama identified those policies as the tax rate cuts and deregulation supported by the Republicans.

But there is no economic theory under which tax rate cuts cause recessions. Even under Keynesian economics, tax rate cuts are expansionary. Even Karl Marx never said tax rate cuts cause economic downturns.

Tax rate cuts are inherently pro-growth because they increase incentives for productive activities by enabling producers to keep a higher percentage of what they produce. The result is greater savings, investment, business start-ups, business expansion, job creation, higher wages, and more economic growth, depending on exactly which tax rates are cut.

That is why when Bush cut the capital gains tax rate from 20 percent to 15 percent in 2003, capital gains tax revenue doubled from 2003 to 2005.[46] By 2006, capital gains revenues were running ahead of pre-tax-cut projections by $133 billion.[47] Similarly, after Bush cut the top tax rate on corporate dividend payments from nearly 40 percent to 15 percent, corporate dividends paid soared, as did the tax revenues paid on those dividend payments.

And that is why after the Bush tax cuts of 2001 and 2003, total annual federal revenues soared, rising between 2000 and 2007 by 27 percent, or more than half-a-trillion dollars.[48] The deficit in the last budget adopted by a Republican majority Congress was $161 billion in 2007.[49] practically balanced compared to Obama's four years of deficits of well over a trillion dollars, which was about eight times as much as the last Republican deficit. The day the Democrat congressional majorities took office, January 3, 2007, the unemployment rate was 4.6 percent.[50]

So how did these rate cuts cause the financial crisis? Obviously, they didn't.

Similarly, after Reagan cut income tax rates across the board by 25 percent in 1981 and then adopted the 1986 tax reform reducing the top income tax rate from 70 percent when he entered office to 28 percent, the economy boomed throughout the 1980s, and federal revenues doubled, despite the rate cuts.[51]

President Kennedy also proposed income tax rate cuts across the board by roughly 25 percent, which were enacted in 1964 after his untimely death. The next year, economic growth soared by 50 percent and income tax revenues increased by 41 percent.[52] By 1966, unemployment had fallen to its lowest peacetime level in almost 40 years. *U.S. News and World Report* exclaimed, "The unusual budget spectacle of sharply rising revenues following the biggest tax cut in history is beginning to astonish even those who pushed hardest for tax cuts in the first place."[53] Arthur Okun, the administration's chief economic advisor, estimated the tax cuts expanded the economy in just two years by 10 percent above where it would have been.[54]

It's also important to recall that Bush was not noteworthy as a deregulator. Political propagandists try to argue the bipartisan repeal of the New Deal-era Glass-Steagall Act in 1999 contributed to the financial crisis. But just the opposite was true. The repeal of hopelessly outdated Glass-Steagall eased the financial crisis by enabling commercial bank holding companies to purchase and rescue failing investment banks. JPMorgan Chase (that is, its holding company), for example, bought out the failing Bear Stearns.

Glass-Steagall was passed to prevent commercial banks taking government-insured deposits from failing due to losses incurred through riskier investment banking activities (issuing stock and other securities). But the 2008 financial crisis did not involve commercial banks failing due to investment banking activities. It involved investment banks failing due to traditional investment-banking activities, such as issuing and holding mortgage-backed securities. Some deposit-taking banks got into trouble due to traditional banking activities, such as making and holding mortgage loans. But that was not prohibited by Glass-Steagall.

Glass-Steagall was repealed so U.S. financial institutions could better compete with European and Japanese universal banks, which were not subject to Glass-Steagall separation. By the time the repeal was enacted, modern financial innovations had created so many loopholes in Glass-Steagall that the distinction between commercial and investment banking could no longer be maintained anyway. That is why President Bill Clinton joined overwhelming bipartisan majorities in Congress to repeal Glass-Steagall.

Even with that repeal, commercial and investment banking could not be formally joined in the same banking corporation. The repeal meant only that a bank holding company, or parent corporation, could own both a commercial bank and an investment bank. Government-insured deposits could not be used to speculate in riskier investment-banking activities. That is why the reform served only to strengthen the financial community and ease the financial crisis.

The roots of the financial crisis began with the overregulation involved in Clinton's National Home Ownership Strategy, announced on June 5, 1995,[55] though some of the same policies had been developing for almost 20 years. The strategy involved more than 100 regulatory initiatives to force banks to abandon their traditional lending standards and create the subprime mortgage market. Included in that effort were a vastly beefed-up Community Reinvestment Act, actual or threatened discrimination suits by the Departments of Justice and Housing and Urban Development to enforce regulatory requirements, and regulatory mandates on Fannie Mae and Freddie Mac to finance trillions of dollars in mortgage securities backed by subprime mortgages. The Democrat idea behind that Clinton policy was that it was unfair for some people to be denied mortgage loans just because they couldn't pay them back, particularly since those denied were disproportionately black or Hispanic, and poor.

The resulting depreciated lending standards spread throughout the mortgage market, including those for higher-income borrowers speculating in second and third homes. Once the lending standards were weakened for those with the lowest incomes and weakest credit, mortgages couldn't be denied to those who were more creditworthy. All this extra mortgage money flowing into housing gave birth to the housing bubble.

The government-sponsored enterprises Fannie Mae and Freddie Mac, created precisely to lead the development of markets in mortgage backed securities, were able to attract trillions of dollars in additional financing from capital markets because their securities were recognized as effectively government-guaranteed. That pumped up the housing bubble further.

In rating these Fannie and Freddie subprime mortgage securities AAA and misleading everybody as to the real risks involved, the leading credit rating agencies failed to do their job. But their ratings enjoyed privileged recognition in regulations governing investments by banks and other financial institutions, protecting them from competition, so the rating agencies had incentives to avoid rocking the boat. This was another problem caused by too much regulation.

Bush also contributed to the crisis. Instead of Reagan's strong-dollar monetary policies that slayed inflation, for years Bush's Treasury secretaries supported weak-dollar monetary policies with even negative real interest rates. Ben Bernanke, a Bush appointee, was already at the Fed in those years promoting monetary deconstruction. That pumped trillions more dollars into the housing bubble and other over-construction as cheap money and record-low interest rates promoted overinvestment in the longest-term alternatives.[56]

Once the housing bubble inevitably burst in 2007 because it grew beyond what could be further supported, all the chickens came home to roost in 2008. Mortgage-backed securities composed of toxic subprime loans had been spread by Fannie Mae and Freddie Mac throughout the world financial community. Major investment banks that overinvested in those securities, further misled by negative real interest rates into massive overleveraging, went bust.

Obama's Failure to Achieve Recovery

Obama's job was to manage a timely, robust recovery from this bust, which was quite possible to do. The situation, after all, was not as bad as the double-digit inflation, double-digit interest rates, soaring unemployment, declining incomes, and persistently rising poverty Reagan faced when he took office. But Obama pursued exactly the opposite of every pro-growth policy pursued by Reagan. Instead of Reagan's lower tax rates, Obama pursued higher tax rates. Instead of cutting spending as Reagan did with his much-vilified budget cuts starting in 1981, Obama started off with a trillion-dollar stimulus that has stimulated nothing except government spending, deficits, and debt. Obama continued from there to become the biggest government spender in world history. Instead of reducing regulatory costs and burdens, Obama has gone wild with new regulatory costs and burdens, from EPA to Dodd-Frank to Obamacare and beyond.

And instead of anti-inflation, strong-dollar monetary policies that make every American holding a dollar richer, Obama led the cheerleading for continued zero-interest-rate, pro-inflation monetary policies that will ultimately make every American holding a dollar poorer.

The result has been the opposite of the results of Reaganomics: the weakest recovery since the Great Depression, with only a third or less of the growth in Reagan's real recovery. As a result, we suffered the longest period with unemployment above 8 percent since the Great Depression. Millions more people have dropped out of the workforce, with the lowest labor participation rate in more than 30 years. Real wages and incomes persisted in falling, even faster after the recession supposedly ended. Median family annual income fell by more than $4,000 in the years after Obama took office, the equivalent of almost a month of lost income annually. Poverty and dependency soared to the highest totals on record. This looks like Carter all over again. The benchmarks Obama has failed to reach are the signposts of previous recoveries.

The Obama economic blunders mentioned above and other Obama policies have only perpetuated the causes of the financial crisis. Obama's regulators have continued to pursue many of the same subprime regulatory policies as Bill Clinton, including the Community Reinvestment Act (which should be repealed), and expanded lending discrimination suits for those banks that try to maintain traditional lending standards in housing and in business lending. The Obama administration also led the cheerleading and maintained political cover for the loose monetary policies of Fed Chairman Ben Bernanke, who perpetuated for years the lowest real interest rates in American history. So Obama has laid the groundwork for renewed recession and financial crisis.

Roadmap to Prosperity

How would we implement the enormously successful policies of Reaganomics today?

Recovery is long overdue for the U.S. economy. The recession began in December 2007, according to the National Bureau of Economic Research (NBER), which is considered the official scorekeeper of when recessions start and end. Since the Great Depression and prior to this latest downturn, recessions in the United States lasted an average of 10 months, with the longest previously being 16 months. But here we are more than seven years after the recession began, and the American people rightly still do not feel like we have ever enjoyed a real recovery.

Yes, the recession technically ended in June 2009. But what we have experienced since then is the worst recovery since the Great Depression, as discussed above. That is the standard by which Obama's economic policies should be judged, by comparison to the recoveries of prior presidents from prior recessions.

Obama apologists can't argue the recovery has been so bad because the recession was so bad. The American historical record is that the worse the recession, the stronger the recovery. Based on that historical record, we should be in the sixth year of a booming recovery by now.

The chief excuse of the Obama apologists is that what we have suffered was not just a recession but a financial crisis, and (they argue) recovery from a financial crisis takes a lot longer than recovery from a recession. But that is not the experience of the free-market, capitalist, U.S. economy, where recessions have lasted roughly a year to at most a year and a half, and the worse the recession the stronger the recovery. That experience of the U.S. economy is reported in full by the National Bureau of Economic Research. That is the standard by which the performance of Obamanomics is logically to be judged.

Obama apologists rely on the book *This Time Is Different: Eight Centuries of Financial Folly*, by Carmen Reinhart and Kenneth S. Rogoff.[57] But that book merely changes the subject, basing its argument on data that "covers sixty-six countries over nearly eight centuries." It "goes back as far as twelfth century China and medieval Europe." The data "come from Africa, Asia, Europe, Latin America, North America, and Oceania."[58]

But that experience does not meet the valid standard of expectations for post-Depression, free-market, capitalist America over the past 70 years, the most powerful economic engine in the history of the world. Obama was elected president of the United States, not twelfth-century China.

Moreover, as explained by economist John Lott at FoxNews.com,[59] the Reinhart-Rogoff thesis about financial crises is not supported by the data. Lott explains that in five of the past six financial crises in economies worldwide, excluding only the Great Depression, booming economic growth during the recovery exceeded the decline in the previous recession by 6 percentage points. So a financial crisis does not preclude a timely, booming recovery.

Lott adds, "Unemployment actually recovered faster in countries hit by a financial crisis than in those in a recession for other reasons. ... From January 2009 to December 2011, the unemployment rates in countries with financial crises actually increased less than in those that avoided such a crisis."[60] He further observes, "Countries identified as suffering a financial crisis by Reinhart and Rogoff also did not experience slower GDP growth during their recoveries."[61]

The real reason Obama's recovery has been the worst since the Great Depression is that he went back to the Keynesian economics of the Great Depression, which didn't work then and won't work now, and has pursued exactly the opposite of every pro-growth policy illuminated by Reagan. Contrary to Keynesian economics, demand is insatiable and can never be inadequate in a market economy. If the demand for any product or service is not strong enough, the price of the good or service will fall, until demand equals supply. The people can never spend more than they produce. And they will never spend less, for they will either consume or save every dime they earn (produce). The consumption goes into consumer spending and the savings go into capital spending, which is what makes us richer and more prosperous.

The U.S. economy has a long-overdue boom already locked within it, straining to break out. Adopting updated policies of Reaganomics would unleash the boom. Here's what needs to be done:

1. Cut Tax Rates through Tax Reform. The first component of those updated policies would be classic tax reform, lowering rates in return for closing loopholes. Obama's tax policies have been essentially the opposite of such tax reform, raising rates to finance new loopholes, especially involving tax credits, where the government dictates certain actions in return for a tax cut reward.

Working under the auspices of Lew Uhler's National Tax Limitation Committee, we convened a group of the nation's top free-market tax experts in Washington to develop the most pro-growth tax reform. The consensus was to refocus our income tax system on consumption, rather than savings and investment, the lifeblood of capitalist economies and the economic foundation for job creation and rising wages and incomes.

That can be accomplished first by allowing all families and individuals to deduct from taxable income all capital investment, savings, debt reduction, and retirement account contributions. Second, allow capital "expensing" for all business, which means replacing depreciation with deductions each year for all expenses for plant and equipment in that year.

For Individuals and Families

The income tax rate structure would be a modified version of the tax reform included in Budget Committee Chairman Paul Ryan's House budgets. That would involve a tax rate of 10 percent on earned income up to the maximum taxable income for the Social Security payroll tax, currently $118,500 for 2015, and 22.4 percent for income above that. Social Security's maximum taxable income is automatically indexed to rise with wages each year, which means that inflation would not push working people into the higher income tax bracket. That means 90 percent of all wages would remain subject only to the 10 percent rate for income taxes.

This would create essentially a flat rate tax for the income tax and the 12.4 percent total Social Security payroll tax combined. Working people would bear a total income tax and Social Security effective tax burden of 22.4 percent on the first $118,500 of wages this year. The 12.4 percent payroll tax would then drop off, but the income tax rate would rise to 22.4 percent for wage income above $118,500 for the year.

The current personal exemption of $3,000 would be raised to $6,000, exempting the first $24,000 annually from income taxes for a family of four. The plan would retain deductions for home mortgage interest and charitable contributions, but eliminate deductions for state and local taxes, which just subsidize state and local tax increases.

Multiple taxation of capital would be addressed by killing the egregious, hated "death tax," and taxing dividends, capital gains and business income at a single rate of 10 percent.

For Corporations

The federal corporate income tax rate would be reduced to 10 percent, as would the capital gains tax and the tax on corporate dividends. That would be close to the revenue-maximizing tax rate. When President Bush cut capital gains from 20 percent to 15 percent in 2003, capital gains revenues soared in the following years.

Such tax reform proposals would promote a new economic boom. America would be first worldwide in business-friendly tax policy, eliminating "tax inversions" and spawning waves of companies, capital ($2 trillion currently sheltered offshore), and jobs flowing back to the United States. Every dollar not taken in taxes from corporations provides about 50¢ for increased wages and jobs, increases earnings of pension funds, and decreases product and service prices.

Such reform was not designed to be "revenue neutral," but a major tax cut under static scoring, though ultimately revenue-positive under dynamic scoring considering the pro-growth effects of the reform. A standard dynamic economic model in fact scored the tax reform as follows: Over the first 10 years, nearly 80 percent of the revenue losses from the dramatic rate cuts would be recovered from the resulting dynamically increased savings, investment, job creation, wage increases, and economic growth.

After 10 years, GDP would be 16 percent higher than otherwise, which means the economy would be producing $2.6 trillion more each year for American families and working people. Wages would be 11 percent higher than otherwise, with 5.2 million more full-time jobs. The net revenue loss after 10 years would be only 2 percent ($111.4 billion) of the then-projected federal budget ($5.9 trillion). The private economy would gain $24 in increased output and production for each dollar of net revenue loss.

2. Cut Spending to Balance the Budget. The federal budget for 2015 proposed by then-House Budget Committee Chairman Paul Ryan, and adopted for the entire House by the Republican majority, would get the federal spending, deficit, and debt problems under control. It would cut $6.8 trillion from spending over the next ten years alone, cutting the deficit by 86 percent in only four years, by 2017, as scored by the CBO, while maintaining all the Bush-era tax cuts.[62] With a booming economy, which would result from the policies recommended here, the budget would be balanced by 2017. By 2022, Ryan's budget would be spending nearly a trillion dollars less per year than the 2015 budget Obama proposed.

Over the longer run, Ryan's budget would reduce federal spending from close to 25 percent of GDP to 15 percent of GDP, slashing the size of the government relative to the economy by close to 40 percent.[63] That is achieved not by future spending cuts but by the long-term effects of Ryan's proposed entitlement reforms if adopted today.

Ryan's budget would essentially solve the national debt problem over the long run as a result. It would immediately stabilize and start reducing federal debt held by the public from 77 percent of GDP in 2013 to 62 percent by 2022, which would by itself stop the debt from producing negative economic effects that would reduce economic growth.[64] The debt would continue on a sharp decline from there as the long-term effects of Ryan's structural entitlement reforms phased in. Debt held by the public would be reduced to 53 percent of GDP by 2030, 38 percent by 2040, and

10 percent by 2050.[65] That means the national debt compared to GDP would be nearly paid off by 2050 and would be eliminated soon thereafter. Under dynamic scoring with a booming economy returning America to its long-term economic growth path, the debt probably would be paid off before then.

The entitlement reforms discussed in this book would reduce federal spending by far more and faster over a generation. After a generation, absent reform, Social Security spending is projected to total 10 percent of GDP all by itself. Through personal accounts, all of that spending would ultimately be shifted to the private sector, and off of the federal budget altogether. Applying the personal accounts to Medicare payroll taxes would, over a generation, shift about one third of the spending on that program to the private sector as well. Along with the Medicare premium support reforms proposed by current House Ways and Means Chairman Paul Ryan, after a generation federal Medicare spending would be half of what it would be otherwise, while liberating seniors to enjoy a better Medicare program than under Obamacare.

Extending the 1996 welfare block grants to all federal means-tested welfare programs would reduce the cost of those programs to about half of what they would be otherwise. Repealing and replacing Obamacare with Patient Power would eliminate all of the federal spending increases of Obamacare.

Consequently, over a generation these entitlement reforms would reduce federal spending to at most half of what it would be otherwise. The rest of Ryan's budget would further contribute to that.

3. Deregulation. The third step is to recreate the Reagan deregulation agenda by repealing the tsunami of increased regulatory costs Obama has let loose that threaten to swamp the economy.

That would involve first turning back the crusade pursued by EPA and the Department of the Interior against reliable, traditional energy sources such as coal, oil, and natural gas. Those regulations constitute what is essentially another tax increase on the economy, hampering manufacturing in particular with high and rapidly rising energy costs.

Reform also would involve repealing EPA's ill-advised global warming (alias climate change) regulations, which would involve still another effective tax increase of trillions of dollars over the long run. Science shows the planet's long-term temperature changes have been overwhelmingly due to natural causes and do not portend any kind of catastrophe, much less a human-caused one.[66] The expected increase in atmospheric carbon dioxide (CO_2) levels over the next century would be beneficial to mankind as more CO_2 in the atmosphere improves crop and plant growth, as would modest warming, especially if it occurs mostly in the winter and in the evenings, as would be expected from a modest increase in CO_2 concentrations. Our present CO_2 concentrations are still below longer-term historical norms despite the Industrial Revolution. Increased CO_2 in this sense is truly "green."

Repealing and replacing Obamacare would likewise turn back a costly regulatory morass. The individual mandate and employer mandate both require people to buy the most-costly health insurance possible, effectively constituting another tax increase of trillions of dollars. The Obamacare regulations impose costly increases on employers who already provide health insurance, and the employer mandate imposes those increases on all other employers, constituting a further tax on employment that our nation cannot afford. The regulations providing for community rating and guaranteed issue have proven records of causing rapidly rising costs,[67] which the mandates will not prevent, and the numerous mandated benefits in Obamacare will further increase costs. The increased demand and reduced supply of health care resulting from Obamacare regulations will further increase costs.

Hundreds of additional regulations on the financial community are still pending under the Dodd-Frank legislation, threatening the consumer and business credit essential to fueling economic recovery. Smaller banks have been closing or merging under this regulatory threat and the financial community is reducing hiring. Dodd-Frank does nothing to address the causes of the financial crisis, and it institutionalizes future big bank bailouts rather than terminating them. It too should be repealed, along with the Community Reinvestment Act, a fundamental cause of the financial crisis.

A complete solution to the problem of federal overregulation would require enactment of the proposed REINS (Regulations of the Executive In Need of Scrutiny) Act. That law would require any federal regulation with an impact of more than $100 million a year on the private economy to receive congressional approval before it becomes effective. That would restore the full legislative powers of the federal government back to the Congress as originally intended, rather than extensive, effective legislation delegated to executive agencies as today.

4. Monetary Reform. Perhaps the most crucial step for restoring booming economic growth and the American Dream is fundamental reform of the Federal Reserve and monetary policy. The Fed's policy of near-zero interest rates for several years now and rapid money creation through quantitative easing, buying up most of the new federal debt issued, are a classic prescription for eventual recreation of the roaring inflation of the 1970s.

Federal legislation should provide for fundamental reform of the Fed, replacing open-ended Fed monetary policy with a strict Price Rule. Under such a rule, the Fed's monetary policy would be guided by prices in real markets, particularly the most policy-sensitive commodity prices such as oil, silver, copper, and other precious metals, but most especially gold, the most policy-sensitive commodity of all, reflecting its traditional, historical role as a store of value and money in itself.

Under such a Price Rule, when those prices started to rise in markets, that would signal the threat of inflation is rising, and the Fed would tighten monetary policy and the money supply. When such sensitive prices started to fall, that would signal the threat of recession or deflation, and the Fed should ease monetary policy. Following such monetary policies would avoid both inflation and deflation, avert cyclical bubbles and recessions, and maintain a stable value of the dollar.

Such a monetary system promotes economic growth because investors know the value of their investments will be maintained without depreciation due to inflation or a declining value of the dollar, and that cyclical recessions that might crash their investments will be minimized. This is the policy the Fed should be mandated by law to follow to promote economic growth and another economic boom.

The best way to enforce such a Price Rule is full gold convertibility at the target price of gold. That would restore a full-blown gold standard. Then anyone anywhere would hold the power to convert a dollar into the quantity of gold equal to a dollar at the Price Rule target price. That would restrain the Fed into following monetary policy that would hold the value of dollar at the target price for gold under the Price Rule.

Note that does not mean the money supply under a gold standard is fixed to any quantity of gold. If the value of the dollar is held stable by monetary policy at the target price of gold, there would be no reason for large exchanges of dollars into gold. The dollars would then be good as gold themselves, and the entire gold standard could be operated on a small amount of actual gold. In other words, the gold standard is not meant to fix the money supply to any particular level. It is meant to hold the value of the dollar stable at the target price for gold, regardless of the amount of gold the government holds.

Conclusion

This proposed restoration of Reaganomics would return the U.S. economy to its long-term economic growth path. That would involve above-normal real economic growth of 4 to 6 percent for several years until the economy returned to its long-term growth path averaging real growth of 3.3 percent per year. That is why deeper recessions result in stronger recoveries, because the economy must go faster than normal for a time to catch up to its long-term historical average. That is what happened with Reagan's historic recovery from the stagflation of the 1970s. Today that would involve the restoration of full employment.

The restoration of that booming economic growth would provide the foundation for successful long-term entitlement reform by maximizing government revenues to cover long-term liabilities, providing more jobs at higher wages to reduce the number of the poor, empowering more people to afford health coverage or get it from their employers, and ensuring that retirement savings and investment would earn robust returns.

But those entitlement reforms themselves would further boost economic growth beyond the long-term economic growth trendline that has made America the richest, most prosperous, most militarily dominant country in world history. Personal accounts for Social Security would produce mighty rivers of increased savings and investment flowing into the economy, on the order of $8 trillion over the first 15 years and $16 trillion over the first 25 years, according to scores by the Chief Actuary of Social Security.

Welfare reform would promote waves of increased labor into the economy to join this increased capital, as a trillion dollars a year paid by taxpayers today to the bottom 20 percent of the income distribution not to work is replaced by far more paid by private employers for those millions of Americans to join the workforce and contribute to the economy. Sharply increased capital plus sharply increased labor in the economy equals economic boom, the most fundamental equation of economics.

Repealing and Replacing Obamacare by Patient Power would further eliminate trillions of dollars in the effective tax burden on the economy imposed by the employer and individual mandates, and the increased health care costs imposed by the Obamacare overregulation, as well as at least a trillion dollars in explicit taxation imposed by the nefarious program over the first 10 years. The effective health care cost controls involved in the market incentives and competition of Patient Power reforms would be another major, effective tax cut for the economy.

That all translates into the very long term restoration of the American Dream.

Notes

1. Brian Domitrovic, *Econoclasts: The Rebels Who Sparked the Supply Side Revolution and Restored American Prosperity* (Wilmington, DE: Intercollegiate Studies Institute, 2009), p. 6.

2. *Ibid.*

3. See Amity Shlaes, *The Forgotten Man: A New History of the Great Depression* (New York, NY: Harper Collins, 2007); Burton Folsom, Jr., *New Deal or Raw Deal?* (New York, NY: Threshold, 2008).

4. Robert Bartley, *The Seven Fat Years* (New York, NY: The Free Press, 1992), p. 112.

5. *Economic Report of the President*, January 1993, Table 13-71, p. 430.

6. *Ibid.*, Table 13-69, p. 428.

7. *Ibid.*, Table B-28, p. 380.

8. *Ibid.*

9. Richard B. McKenzie, *What Went Right in the 1980s* (San Francisco, CA: Pacific Research Institute for Public Policy, 1994), p. 102.

10. Alan Reynolds, "Upstarts and Downstarts," in "The Real Reagan Record," *National Review*, August 31, 1992, p. 26.

11. *Ibid.* pp. 25–6.

12. *Ibid.*, p. 3.

13. Brian Domitrovic, *supra* note 1.

14. Peter Ferrara, "When the Republicans Cut Spending," *American Spectator*, September 2008.

15. *Ibid.*

16. *Ibid.*

17. *Ibid.*

18. Robert Bartley, *supra* note 4, pp. 135, 144.

19. *Ibid.*

20. *Ibid.*, p. 4; Richard McKenzie, *supra* note 9, p. 8.

21. Arthur B. Laffer, Stephen Moore, and Peter J. Tanous, *The End of Prosperity* (New York, NY: Simon & Schuster, 2008), p. 88.

22. *Economic Report of the President*, *supra* note 5, Table B-32, p. 385.

23. *Ibid.*, Table 13-69, p. 428.

24. Robert Bartley, *supra* note 4, p. 4.

25. Robert McKenzie, *supra* note 9, p. 102.

26. *Economic Report of the President, supra* note 5, Table B-28, p. 380.

27. *Ibid.*, Table 13-59, p. 462.

28. *Ibid.*

29. *Ibid.*, Table 13-69, p. 428.

30. *Ibid.*

31. Richard McKenzie, *supra* note 9, pp. 7, 187.

32. *Ibid.*, p. 183.

33. *Economic Report of the President, supra* note 5, Table B-110, p. 473.

34. Arthur B. Laffer, Stephen Moore, and Peter J. Tanous, *supra* note 21, p. 89.

35. *Ibid.*, p. 3.

36. Steve Forbes, "How Capitalism Will Save Us," *Forbes*, November 10, 2008.

37. Dan Clifton, "The Economic and Fiscal Impact of the 2003 Tax Cut," American Shareholders Association, April 2007.

38. *Ibid.*

39. *Ibid.*

40. *Ibid.*

41. *Ibid.*

42. *Ibid.*

43. *Ibid.*

44. Henry R. Nau, "Lessons from the Great Expansion," *The Wall Street Journal*, January 26, 2012.

45. *Ibid.*

46. Dan Clifton, *supra* note 37.

47. *Ibid.*

48. Office of Management and Budget, *The President's Budget for Fiscal Year 2013*, Historical Tables, Table 1.1, Summary of Receipts, Outlays, and Surpluses or Deficits, 1789–2015.

49. *Ibid.*

50. Bureau of Labor Statistics.

51. Office of Management and Budget, *supra* note 48.

52. Arthur B. Laffer, Stephen Moore, and Peter J. Tanous, *supra* note 21.

53. *Ibid.*

54. *Ibid.*

55. Stan J. Liebowitz, "Anatomy of a Train Wreck: Causes of the Mortgage Meltdown," The Independent Institute, *Independent Policy Report*, October 3, 2008, p. 10.

56. John B. Taylor, *Getting Off Track* (Stanford, CA: Hoover Institution Press, 2009).

57. Carmen M. Reinhart and Kenneth Rogoff, *This Time Is Different: Eight Centuries of Financial Folly* (Princeton, NJ: University Press, 2009).

58. *Ibid.*

59. John Lott, Jerry Dwyer, and James Lothian, "The Financial Crisis Can't Explain the Slow Recovery," Fox News, November 5, 2012.

60. *Ibid.*

61. *Ibid.*

62. The Path To Prosperity," United States House Budget Committee, March 20, 2012, http://budget.house.gov/uploadedfiles/pathtoprosperity2013.pdf.

63. *Ibid.*

64. *Ibid.*

65. *Ibid.*

66. Craig Idso and S. Fred Singer, *Climate Change Reconsidered: 2009 Report of the Nongovernmental International Panel on Climate Change (NIPCC)* (Chicago, IL: The Heartland Institute, 2009); Craig D. Idso, Robert M. Carter, and S. Fred Singer, eds., *Climate Change Reconsidered: 2011 Interim Report of the Nongovernmental International Panel on Climate Change (NIPCC)* (Chicago, IL: The Heartland Institute, 2011); Craig D. Idso, Robert M. Carter, and S. Fred Singer, *Climate Change Reconsidered II: Physical Science*, (Chicago, IL: The Heartland Institute, 2013).

67. Conrad F. Meier, *Destroying Insurance Markets: How Guaranteed Issue and Community Rating Destroyed the Individual Health Insurance Market in Eight States* (Alexandria, VA and Chicago, IL: Council for Affordable Health Insurance and The Heartland Institute, 2005).

About the Author

Peter Ferrara is senior fellow for entitlement and budget policy at The Heartland Institute, a senior fellow at the National Center for Policy Analysis, senior policy advisor on entitlements and budget policy for the National Tax Limitation Foundation, and general counsel of the American Civil Rights Union.

He served in the White House Office of Policy Development under President Ronald Reagan and as associate deputy attorney general of the United States under President George H.W. Bush. He is a graduate of Harvard College and Harvard Law School. He is author of many books including *The Obamacare Disaster* (Chicago, IL: The Heartland Institute, 2010), *President Obama's Tax Piracy* (Jackson, TN: Encounter Books, 2010), and *America's Ticking Bankruptcy Bomb: How the Looming Debt Crisis Threatens the American Dream – and How We Can Turn the Tide Before It's Too Late* (New York, NY: Broadside Books, June 2011).

About the Publisher

The Heartland Institute is a national nonprofit research and education organization. Founded in Chicago, Illinois in 1984, Heartland's mission is to discover, develop, and promote free-market solutions to social and economic problems. Its activities are tax-exempt under Section 501(c)(3) of the Internal Revenue Code.

Heartland is headquartered in Chicago, Illinois and has a full-time staff of 34 and a 2014 budget of approximately $7 million. It is supported by the voluntary contributions of approximately 5,500 supporters. For more information, please visit our website at www.heartland.org; write to us at 3939 North Wilke Road, Arlington Heights, IL 60004, or call 312/377-4000.